Defying the Odds

Defying the Odds

Class and the Pursuit of Higher Literacy

Donna Dunbar-Odom

State University of New York Press

Published by
STATE UNIVERSITY OF NEW YORK PRESS
ALBANY

© 2007 State University of New York

All rights reserved

Printed in the United States of America

For information, address
State University of New York Press
194 Washington Avenue, Suite 305, Albany, NY 12210-2384

Production by Ryan Hacker
Marketing by Susan M. Petrie

Library of Congress Cataloging-in-Publication Data

Dunbar-Odom, Donna.
    Defying the odds : class and the pursuit of higher literacy / Donna Dunbar-Odom.
    p. cm.
    Includes bibliographical references and index.
    ISBN-13: 978-0-7914-6971-2 (hardcover : alk. paper)
    ISBN-13: 978-0-7914-6972-9 (pbk : alk. paper)
    1. Literacy—Social aspects—United States.   2. Social classes—United States.   I. Title.

LC151.D86 2007
302.2'244—dc22   2006007113

10   9   8   7   6   5   4   3   2   1

Contents

Acknowledgments

THIS BOOK HAS DEEP ROOTS.

Of course, I cannot claim any grand epiphanies, but I can recall a number of contributing moments. For example, the experience of working with basic writing students at an open admissions university taught me far more than I was able to teach the students. They taught me about learning, certainly, but I also learned priceless lessons about pedagogy and politics.

Another moment came at my first Conference on College Composition and Communication where I found myself attending a panel on basic writing, listening to presentations by David Bartholomae and Mariolina Salvatori. Rarely can we say that a conference panel has much real effect on us, but this one literally changed my life since I ended up going to the University of Pittsburgh for my doctorate. The work I did there introduced me to ways of teaching and "ways of reading" that have shaped me profoundly, and I am grateful. In particular, the Literacy and Pedagogy seminar with Mariolina Salvatori and my fellow students is where *Defying the Odds* began to develop in earnest.

Here at Texas A&M University-Commerce I have been lucky once more to find myself working with wonderful people: Bill Bolin, Liz Buckley, Gerald Duchovnay, and Dick Fulkerson have been great colleagues. Shannon Carter read every word of this manuscript more than once and is an invaluable friend and colleague. I am also grateful to my students, particularly the following students who generously allowed me to use excerpts from their writing in this project: Catherine Canzoneri, Kimberly Dunham, Marcus Lane, Michael, Nick Monday, and Julie Watson; Mark Abelson, Mallory Baptiste, Elissa Daniel, Roderigo Echeverria, Steve Huffer, Sean Kennedy, Axa Lima, Jackie Nenninger, Rachel Nichols, Kim Pacheco, and Evan Teer; and Scott Lancaster, Mike Marlow, Connie Meyer, Paul Mooney, and Terry Peterman.

Two friendships that began at Pitt continue to sustain me now. Barbara McCarthy and Richard Miller make me think and laugh, and they never let me forget what is important about the work we do. At the same time they accomplish some of the smartest work being done in the academy currently.

vii

SUNY Press has made *Defying the Odds* a real labor of love. I did not know it was possible for the production of a book to be so pleasurable and anxiety-free. My gratitude goes to James Peltz, Larin McLaughlin, Ryan Hacker, Anne Valentine, Therese Myers, and Ken Schrider. I would also like to thank the anonymous readers for their thoughtful and generous reviews. And I am grateful to Wendy Griffiths at the Modern Art Museum of Fort Worth for her help in allowing me to use an image of Anselm Kiefer's *Book with Wings* for the cover, a work that has resonated powerfully for me since I first saw it.

Finally, I want to thank Michael and Claire Odom. My real education began by watching and learning from Mike how to read with rigor and pleasure. I would not have made it through any level of college and beyond without his intellectual and emotional support. He is my ally in every sense of the word. My education continues with Claire whom I watch in awe as she moves through the world with intelligence, humor, and grace.

Chapter One

Situating Literacy

In the Modern Art Museum of Fort Worth stands a lead sculpture, a giant open book with enormous wings sprouting from either side, standing on an a tall pedestal. Anselm Kiefer's *Book with Wings* offers multiple readings: literacy promises to free us—the flight of imagination, for example—but materiality can never be overcome. Kiefer's choice of a medium is not accidental; he could have produced the sculpture in aluminum or wood or even paper, so the choice of lead is significant. In other words, literacy can only give us the illusion of freedom as we remain weighted, inexorably, to our material lives. We want to believe that flight or escape is available through literacy, but when we look up from the page, we are the same people in the same bodies in the same circumstances. Yet literacy has had enormous impact on individuals as published testimonials attest.

American culture, of course, invests heavily in the notion that literacy will free us from poverty, from prejudice, from oppression. But the United States is not the only culture or cultural body to hold to this belief. The United Nations has produced research that maintains a nation must achieve a certain literacy level among its population before it can begin to rise economically. As Sylvia Scribner's "Literacy in Three Metaphors" shows, these assumptions about literacy have helped shape public policy: "In a contemporary framework, expansion of literacy skills is often viewed as a means for poor and politically powerless groups to claim their place in the world" (75). Increased literacy is also assumed to be necessary for a person's ability to think abstractly. Scribner writes, "An individual who is illiterate, a UNESCO (1972) publication states, is bound to concrete thinking and cannot learn new material" (77). Scribner's research among the Vai people in Western Africa, however, then goes on to disprove these assumptions as her five-year study of Vai literacy and literate practices reveal the value-laden nature of Western definitions and reveal as well how literacy in practice cannot be neatly contained by either definitions or metaphors. One would hope that, given the datedness of these references, they would no longer have currency; however, many still widely believe that literacy is a guarantee of national as well as individual success.

But, as Robert F. Arnove and Harvey J. Graff point out in "National Literacy Campaigns," literacy does not automatically lead to anything by itself; to make social or economic change possible, it has to be part of a nexus of factors to have significant effect:

> To ask of literacy that it overcome gender discrimination, integrate a society, eliminate inequalities, and contribute to political and social stability is certainly too much. Ultimately, the retention and uses of literacy depend on the context of the environment of opportunities available to people to use their literacy skills, transformations in social structures, and the ideology of leaders. Whether the materials and methods of literacy and postliteracy campaigns are truly designed to equip people to play more active roles in shaping the direction of their society or, to the contrary, are intended to induct people into roles predetermined by others is a telling indicator of ideology and intent. (614)

In other words, literacy's efficacy is contextual, and the expectations we have regarding what literacy can and cannot make possible are largely ideological. More recently, Deborah Brandt's *Literacy in American Lives* offers case studies of eighty Americans of varying ages and from various socioeconomic, ethnic, and racial backgrounds to disrupt assumptions about literacy's power to change personal and economic circumstances. As Kiefer's sculpture shows, being literate is neither a simple nor a straightforward process. Brandt writes:

> Expanding literacy undeniably has been an instrument for more democratic access to learning, political participation, and upward mobility. At the same time, it has become one of the sharpest tools for stratification and denial of opportunities. Print in the twentieth century was the sea on which ideas and other cultural goods flowed easily among regions, occupations, and social classes. But it also was a mechanism by which the great bureaucracies of modern life tightened around us, along with their systems of testing, sorting, controlling, and coercing. (2)

At the same time literacy makes social and economic mobility possible, it also provides the means to determine standards for what sorts of literate practices will and will not allow access to that mobility. In addition, Brandt reveals those standards to be fluid: "Unending cycles of competition and change keep raising the stakes for literacy achievement" (2). In other words, economic and social mobility require increasingly higher levels of literacy, and definitions of what being literate means are not stable.

At this point, I should explain how I am defining literacy within this project. As a teacher of first-year writing on the college level, I am not, of course, talking about the rudimentary decoding of letters. Despite elitist jeremiads of declining skills and abilities, first-year students come to college able to read and write. The kind or level of literacy that concerns me is the ability to read and make critical judgments about a variety of texts and then to communicate those judgments in writing. In other words, I am referring to a fairly high level of literacy—"higher" literacy if you will. I am also borrowing from Brian V. Street's definition that stresses literacy as "the social practices and conceptions of reading and writing" (1). As with Arnove and Graff, he also argues that literacy is context- and ideology-bound; he "contend[s] that what the particular practices and concepts of reading and writing are for a given society depends upon the context; that they are already embedded in an ideology and cannot be isolated or treated as 'neutral' or merely 'technical'" (1).

My concern in writing this book is not with judging what constitutes successful literate practices; my concern is with the why of literate behavior—specifically, why do some of us pursue higher literacy with almost single-minded devotion. In particular, I am interested in viewing higher literacy through the lens of class. My interest arises from my twenty-plus years as a teacher of composition who continues to be puzzled by why some students succeed and others fail. My interest is further complicated and motivated by my own literacy history as a child of working-class parents whose interests in higher literacy were minimal and who found my passion for increased literacy and higher education perplexing at best. I have to wonder where my intense desire to read and study increasingly complex texts comes from because it was not significantly encouraged in my early years. In fact, being utterly absorbed in a book, as opposed to flipping through a magazine or newspaper, was perceived as a cause for concern. Too much reading was ruining my eyes. Too much reading was not "good" for me. My mother refused to teach me to read or even to write my name before I started school in the first grade. She was not being abusive or cruel; she just did not want me to be ahead of my classmates because, to her way of thinking, standing out and being "different" was not a good thing. I was nurtured by teachers along the way, but, quite honestly, I can only remember being praised by teachers twice in twelve years of public school, and I distinctly remember feeling uncomfortable on both occasions at being singled out—at being "different."

So my desire for higher literacy is rooted in the personal. My motivation is not merely to analyze and work through my own anxieties and unresolved psychological baggage—at least I hope it is not—but research questions, much like medical specialties, arise from a personal experience or connection. In addition, in composition studies, we continue to experience the allure of the personal. (I address recent scholarly attention to the "personal" in our teaching and writing in chapter 4.) We reject current-traditional methods that divide reading and writing assignments into modes and begin with personal narratives, but we still feel the pull of personal narrative. Robert E. Coles argues that we are "called" by stories, and Joseph Trimmer says, "To narrate is to know" (xv). Trimmer continues, "We need to tell our teaching stories if we are to understand our teaching lives" (xv). Although telling stories does not necessarily lead to "understanding," stories do provide an important site of knowledge both for us and for our students, and the site becomes richer when we bring the stories together.

Of course, stories drawn from our experience are not enough in themselves. Just relating experience does nothing to situate it within a culture; just telling a story does nothing toward making sense of the role it plays within that culture. In "Deep Play: Notes on the Balinese Cockfight," Clifford Geertz writes:

> The culture of a people is an ensemble of texts, themselves ensembles, which the anthropologist strains to read over the shoulders of those to whom they properly belong. There are enormous difficulties in such an enterprise, methodological pitfalls to make a Freudian quake, and some moral perplexities as well. Nor is it the only way that symbolic forms can be sociologically handled. Functionalism lives, and so does psychologism. But to regard such forms as "saying something of something," and saying it to somebody, is at least to open up the possibility of an analysis which attends to their substance rather than to reductive formulas professing to account for them. (255)

Geertz's essay attempts to understand the role cockfighting plays in Balinese society. He acknowledges the difficulty an outsider who "strains to read over the shoulders of those to whom they properly belong" faces. His goal is to interpret the experience of others, to open up their experience to analysis. Such interpretation is subject to "methodological pitfalls," but those acts of interpretation allows us to read a culture's "ensemble of texts" with greater complexity and with the potential for alternative readings that can help the reader move beyond prejudice and stereotype.

Sometimes, however, an insider's knowledge is a necessary first step to open the way to those alternative readings. I am reminded of Frederick Douglass's reinterpretation of slave songs in each of his autobiographies. Whereas white people had "read" slaves' singing ("straining to read over their shoulders" if you will) as signifying joy, Douglass makes clear that these interpretations are serious misreadings of this particular "ensemble of texts." What white people had interpreted as joy was actually slaves' misery within slavery and their profound, even unconscious, desire for freedom, argues Douglass. He writes, "I have often been utterly astonished, since I came to the north, to find persons who could speak of the singing, among slaves, as evidence of their contentment and happiness. It is impossible to conceive of a greater mistake. Slaves sing most when they are unhappy" (*Frederick Douglass* 29). Yet Douglass argues that he himself could only comprehend that unhappiness after his escape to freedom. From within the experience, he was too close to read it; only by looking over his own shoulder, to paraphrase Geertz once more, is he able to apprehend the experience of slave songs.

In *Alice Doesn't*, Teresa de Lauretis defines experience as:

the process by which, for all social beings, subjectivity is constructed. Through that process one places oneself or is placed in social reality and so perceives and comprehends as subjective (referring to, originating in oneself) those relations—material, economic, and interpersonal—which are in fact social, and, in a larger perspective, historical. (159)

In other words, experience appears to be individually known and felt; that is, this is my experience of love unlike anyone else's. But how much of the "unique" experience of love is marketed and made consumable (weddings, after all, are part of a multimillion dollar industry)? Consider, too, how difficult resisting or even imagining a love "story" outside a Hollywood narrative is. Experience, too, according to de Lauretis, has history; that is, one can examine the experience of love historically: how definitions of love have evolved, how notions of appropriate partners have changed, and so forth. One way to analyze experience is to look at transgressive acts that challenge the limits of what is being experienced. For example, what can be learned of the experience of love when we consider past laws prohibiting interracial marriage or the current debate regarding gay marriage? Our definitions have to shift—or harden—when we take the "exceptional" into account.

Historian Joan W. Scott points in her article "Experience" to the power of the transgressive or the exceptional to begin a process of understanding experience historically. She begins her essay with a discussion of science fiction writer Samuel Delany's autobiographical narrative in which he describes his first visit to a gay bathhouse. The scene operates to introduce the metaphor of "visibility," that is, of making visible that which has previously been invisible or "outing." Delany's experience "dramatically raises the problem of writing the history of difference, the history, that is, of the designation of 'other,' of the attribution of characteristics that distinguish categories of people from some presumed (and usually unstated) norm" (22). Certainly, rendering the "other" visible is an important step that makes efforts to look away or ignore difference more problematic. And it is a step toward de-exoticizing or demystifying the other. For instance, Douglass's rereading of the slaves' songs make his readers' interpretation of them on a superficial level more difficult to do ever again. They at least have to consider other possible interpretations, and their assumptions have been "troubled."

Still referring to Delany's narrative as her central example, Scott writes:

> We come to appreciate the consequences of the closeting of homosexuals and we understand repression as an interested act of power or domination; alternative behaviors and institutions also become available to us. What we don't have is a way of placing those alternatives within the framework of (historically contingent) dominant patterns of sexuality and the ideology that supports them. We know they exist, but not how they've been constructed; we know their existence offers a critique of normative practices, but not the extent of the critique. Making visible the experience of a different group exposes the existence of repressive mechanisms, but not their inner workings or logics; we know that difference exists, but we don't understand it as consti-tuted relationally. For that we need to attend to the historical processes that, through discourse, position subjects and produce their experiences. It is not individuals who have experience, but subjects who are constituted through experience. Experience in this definition then becomes not the origin of our explanation, not the authoritative (because seen or felt) evidence that grounds what is known, but rather that which we seek to explain, that about which knowledge is produced. (25–26)

So "otherness" reveals something about the repressive function of the "norm," but it reveals nothing about how the norm functions as repressive. Only by examining both the "norm" and the "other" historically can we begin to under-stand how both are "constituted relationally." Experience is not authoritative evidence; the experience is what we are trying to explain. Or as Scott states later in the same article, "Experience is at once always already an interpretation *and* is in need of interpretation" (37, author's italics). In trying to understand more of the complex relationships people have with literacy, then, we should not accept the assumption that the experience of literacy is "life changing," but instead attempt to understand the larger historical and cultural narrative that would allow such an assumption to emerge. I am not denying that Anna Quindlen experienced literacy in this way as she describes it in her short book *How Read-ing Changed My Life*; I am saying that her interpretation of her experience is available to our interpretation. Experience is bigger than the individual. As teachers, we are in the perfect position to begin that interpretation.

Then, too, I am aware of the problematic nature of my use of "we." Who is this "we" I keep including in my arguments? Certainly, I do not believe that all composition teachers are the same, teach the same, theorize the same, and so forth. I am using the second person plural as an enabling fiction as I argue for certain ways of considering and valuing students and their writing. I am including those teachers who share with me a belief that the students in our classes come in with important things to say and to teach us but that learning to hear those things is a never-completed process.

I should also say something about what I mean when I refer to "students" as well. I hope I am clear that I am not referring to generic students or assuming that all students are the same from one coast to the other. The students who populate the classes I teach are more likely to be first-generation college students and are more likely to be working part-time and commuting. About 14% of our student body is African American, which is a larger percentage than most state colleges and universities in my state, particularly the flagship schools. The percentage of Chicano and Latino students fluctuates, but it is generally around 4% to 6%. The majority of our student population tends to live within a one- to two-hour drive from home even if they live on campus. Many are, in Alfred Lubrano's term, "straddlers"; that is, they come from working-class homes but strive to be middle class. In his book *Limbo: Blue-Collar Roots, White-Collar Dreams*, he writes that straddlers "were born to blue-collar families and then, like me, moved into the strange new territory of the middle class. They are the first in their families to have graduated from college. As such, they straddle two worlds, many of them not feeling at home in either, living in a kind of American limbo" (2). The students in my classes also tend to be politically and religiously conservative, and they generally exhibit little awareness or interest about national or international events. Even the war with Iraq has generated little discussion except among those with loved ones in the armed services. More than 50% of our students identify their religion as Baptist. These students tend to be resigned about reading and writing rather than passionate, but they tend to be good sports about fulfilling these assignments. I rely heavily on the verb "tend" in my description because, of course, these are the broadest of descriptive strokes.

Ignoring class on my campus would be easy—as it most likely would be on most campuses—because students do not want to talk about it and because the divisions are perhaps less evident for students at the university where I teach as they were for me at the "suitcase college" I attended, a college much like this one. But Lubrano argues, "By ignoring class distinctions, people may be overlooking important parts of themselves and failing to understand who they really are. They are Straddlers in limbo, still attached to their working-class roots while living a new kind of life in the white-collar world" (5). When students leave this school, they will be better prepared for the inequities they will likely encounter if class has been frankly discussed. In addition, they may find themselves unprepared for the tensions that can arise between them and loved ones if and when their education begins to change them. Lubrano uses the metaphor of the hinge on a door to describe the straddler's position between worlds:

very true. [handwritten marginal note]

> Being the white-collar child of a blue-collar parent means being the hinge on the door between two ways of life. With one foot in the working class, the other in the middle class, people like me are Straddlers, at home in neither world, living a limbo life. It's the part of the American Dream you may have never heard about: the costs of social mobility. People pay with their anxiety about their place in life. It's a discomfort many never overcome. (8)

I see students trying to live in both worlds and see the toll it takes. My colleagues complain about the "bizarre" excuses our students have for their absences, but the excuses make perfect sense to me, a fellow straddler. My middle-class colleague shakes her head in disgust when a student misses class to take an aunt to a doctor's appointment or to support a sibling in a child custody hearing. But these students are trying simultaneously to be students and to meet their obligations to family members. They come from families who may be pleased that their sons or daughters are working to improve their economic and employment status, but the hard-and-fast rule is that family comes first.

But, of course, the goal is to become middle class; however, how can one know what it means to be middle class if one has had little experience of it apart from what appears on television? As I saw the way my father was treated by the company for which he worked for more than thirty years, I vowed that I would do everything I could to make sure I could never receive the same treatment. Many straddlers are motivated similarly. "But," writes Lubrano, "we don't want to have to totally reject who we are and where we came from to become educated and live in nicer houses. There is, then, unease in the transition, because Straddlers are making a difficult journey. That trip is invisible to the middle class, who don't have to cross class lines to become educated" (82). My middle-class colleague can only interpret her student's absence to help his sister move as a way to get out of coming to class or as a case of insufficient dedication to his education. She cannot see how the student is indeed trying to serve two masters.

Of course, most of the straddlers on my campus do not consider themselves to be working class. In fact, what surprises me most on my campus (although it probably should not) is the extent to which virtually all students, no matter their race or ethnicity, identify as middle class. Of course, I understand that this is the class to which they aspire, the reason they are in college in the first place for most. Based on my own experience, too, I should not be surprised because it did not occur to me to consider myself "working class" or, perhaps more accurately, to consider my background working class until I already had a master's degree, had my first university teaching job, and had heard someone else refer to my background as working class. My family, too, identified as middle class, even though for much of my childhood my father was a milkman and my mother worked hourly wage jobs. Although I can now easily list a dozen or so class markers that clearly reveal my family's working-class status, we did not perceive those tastes, traits, and activities to be markers of any kind. And, as Lubrano points out, "Class can hold you back, or limit you. But if you express this, it sounds like whining" (4). No one wants to be perceived as a whiner, especially if you come from a family like mine, where whining was never rewarded with anything positive.

In *Unequal Childhoods: Class, Race, and Family Life,* Annette Lareau writes, ". . . Americans are much more comfortable recognizing the power of individual initiative [rather] than recognizing the power of social class. Studies show that Americans generally believe that responsibility for their accomplishments rests on their individual efforts" (7). As Lareau states, Americans want to believe their achievements come solely by way of their hard work and perseverance. A colleague of mine told me about a young white male student in her introduction to multicultural literacy class. He expressed displeasure at the focus on difference and at what he perceived as reverse discrimination, more specifically, "white male bashing." In a written assignment, he argued that he had worked for and earned everything he had achieved and that when he finished his college degree, he would begin his job as a vice president in his stepfather's company because he had worked for it. Nothing could convince him that he had any kind of advantage for that job. We can laugh or roll our eyes at what we see as the absurdity of his position, but his beliefs remain firm, and he is not alone in those beliefs. Of course, Americans cannot deny that poverty exists, yet, rather than ask questions of the system that engenders poverty, we have a tendency to blame poverty on those who are poor—particularly poor whites. In the introduction to their book *White Trash: Race and Class in America,* Matt Wray and Annalee Newitz write:

> In a country so steeped in the myth of classlessness, in a culture where we are often at a loss to explain or understand poverty, the white trash stereotype serves as a useful way of blaming the poor for being poor. The term *white trash* helps solidify for the middle and upper classes a sense of cultural and intellectual superiority. (1)

If we assume that with enough hard work no one has to be poor, we can take the next step and assume that those who are poor deserve it.

Despite many Americans' class blindness or prejudice, class does, of course, affect us. Andrew Milner in *Class* writes:

> There are differences in the levels of cultural salience that attach to social class in different national cultures. . . . But the available sociological evidence clearly shows class position to be a primary determinant of cultural behaviour, attitudes, and lifestyle, irrespective of this general level of "awareness" of

class. Indeed, empirical sociological research is so invariant in its findings on this subject so as to call into question the further point of continued speculation about the supposed "death of class." (11–12)

Whether we acknowledge it or not or, as in the case of my family, whether we are even aware of it, class marks us. When I entered college, I truly believed that one college was as good as another. I knew some of the people I went to high school with went to elite private colleges, but it simply never occurred to me that they might gain some advantage by going there instead of the mega-university that I chose for reasons of cost and convenience. I had heard of Harvard and Yale, of course, but schools like that seemed to be from a different universe and to be for the upper classes. Only by looking back, reminiscent of Douglass's ability to "read" slave songs after he was no longer in a position to sing them, can I see how I was marked by my social class. In other words, I exhibited no class consciousness.

What interests me now is how these class divisions and distinctions are maintained and resisted. If we see class distinctions as serving the capitalist state, we can turn to Louis Althusser for a Marxist analysis. Whereas Marx demystified the seemingly "natural" movement of capital, Louis Althusser analyzed the seemingly "natural" operations of state and government in support of capital. Building from Marx's work, Althusser's "Ideology and Ideological State Apparatuses (Notes towards an Investigation)" details how institutions and ideology enmesh to reproduce and maintain stratifications that make possible the continuation of capitalist society: "As Marx said, every child knows that a social formation which did not reproduce the conditions of production at the same time as it produced would not last a year. The ultimate condition of production is therefore the reproduction of the conditions of production" (127). For the capitalist state to continue, it must make possible an endless circulation of capital; production requires the incessant renewal of the means of production. This is true not only in terms of raw materials, but also in terms of labor power and the social formations that produce and sustain it:

> To put this more scientifically, I shall say that the reproduction of labour power requires not only a reproduction of its skills, but also, at the same time, a reproduction of its submission to the rules of the established order, i.e. a reproduction of submission to the ruling ideology for the workers, and a reproduction of the ability to manipulate the ruling ideology correctly for the agents of exploitation and repression, so that they, too, will provide for the domination of the ruling class "in words." (132–33)

For Althusser, then, school is where labor learns to follow the rules and where management learns to enforce them, and there is no possibility for "radical" or "liberatory" education. At this stage in the development of capital, the kind of labor that Marx and Althusser imagined is in non–U.S. countries, so the need for schools to reproduce "submission to the rules" may be even more crucial for capitalism.

According to Althusser, the school functions as an ideological state apparatus (ISA), one of the many ideological state apparatuses including the church, the law, trade unions, and others, not to be confused with the "(repressive) state apparatus," which functions "massively and predominantly by repression (including physical repression), while functioning secondarily by ideology," for example, the police or the military (145). Althusser is careful to point out that the (repressive) state apparatus makes use of ideology to support the means and threat of repression just as ISAs can ultimately take recourse in repression because no apparatus functions as purely repressive or purely ideological.

From this point of view, school is the most important ISA if for no other reason than that students are placed in the system when they are at their most impressionable and kept for six to eight hours a day, five or more days a week for a number of years:

> But it is by an apprenticeship in a variety of know-how wrapped up in the massive inculcation of the ideology of the ruling class that the *relations of production* in a capitalist social formation, i.e. the relations of exploited to exploiters and exploiters to exploited, are largely reproduced. The mechanisms which produce this vital result for the capitalist regime are naturally covered up and concealed by a universally reigning ideology of the School, universally reigning because it is one of the essential forms of the ruling bourgeois ideology: an ideology which represents the School as a neutral environment purged of ideology . . . , where teachers respectful of the "conscience" and "freedom" of the children who are entrusted to them (in complete confidence) by their "parents" (who are free, too, i.e., the owners of their children) open up for them the path to the freedom, morality and responsibility of adults by their own example, by knowledge, literature and their "liberating" virtues. (156–57, author's italics)

His sarcasm notwithstanding, Althusser argues that the public school's pretensions to neutrality and egalitarianism make it such a formidable agent for ideology. Few would argue that schools in areas with a wealthier tax base are better than those from poor neighborhoods, and the disparity has reached a point where it could no longer be ignored. President Bush's No Child Left Behind initiative seemingly eliminates this disparity, offering parents in poor neighborhoods the opportunity to place their children in better schools, but, of course, the reality is that many of these parents have no means to transport their children to better schools and that the better schools do not welcome these students if they do manage to transfer. And the initiative does nothing to address the reasons for the disparity; instead, the assumption is that testing will spawn the means for improvement and success. In other words, No Child Left Behind is the illusion of reform; the status quo is untouched. (For a clear and systematic critique of state-mandated testing, see Gerald Coles's *Reading the Naked Truth: Literacy, Legislation, and Lies.*)

Althusser's argument is reflected in Samuel Bowles and Herbert Gintis's understanding of the school as the "apprentice" period when individuals learn to take their place in the workforce, as "exploiters" or "exploited," having unknowingly absorbed the ideology of the "ruling class." This absorption, however, is accomplished from within the framing metaphors of "freedom" and "liberation." The school, as Althusser points out, is perceived as ideology-free, and teachers see themselves and are seen by others as models exemplifying the ideals, the "'liberating' virtues," of knowledge and literature without, of course, imposing their own political sensibilities on the children in their classes. Figured within Althusser's constructs, parents expect, and even demand, the school's political "neutrality" under the assumption that their bourgeois ideology is simultaneously unique (this is what our family believes is right and true) and natural (this is the way everyone should live). Furthermore, individuals are "free" to choose their own way of living, but that choice ("informed" choice, if you will) is made possible through the "'liberating' virtues" of knowledge and literature, ineffable virtues that transcend mere know-how.

Many educators have worked to expose the "hidden curriculum" that teaches students not to think but to accept their place in capitalist society. Bowles and Gintis, for example, write:

> [W]e suggest that major aspects of educational organization replicate the relationships of dominance and subordinancy in the economic sphere. The correspondence between the social relation of schooling and work accounts for the ability of the educational system to produce an amenable and fragmented labor force. The experience of schooling, and not merely the content of formal learning, is central to this process. (125)

According to Bowles and Gintis, the primary concern of schooling is not what we learn but that we learn our place within the capitalist mode of production. We learn to be "amenable," to submit to and even cooperate with the system that oppresses us, but we are also "fragmented" in that we do not recognize or seek a commonality of purpose that would question or disturb the "relations of dominance and subordinancy in the economic sphere" by means of collective action.

Althusser offers little hope for resistance to the capitalist "regime." Later in his essay he states that the subject is created by ideology: "... *the category of the subject is only constitutive of all ideology insofar as all ideology has the function (which defines it) of 'constituting' concrete individuals as subjects*" (171, author's italics). Society creates the individual as a subject to participate in society and to serve it. Resistance, the ability to recognize ideology as repressive and act autonomously to change or subvert it, seemingly has no opportunity to emerge from this process of the constitution of the individual as a subject because that subject acquires systems of values and codes of behavior, ontology, and morality through ideology. Althusser offers no suggestion as to what allows the subject—such as himself—to see the contradictions of bourgeois ideology, much less act on them. Still he salutes the few teachers with enough courage to fight against the "ruling bourgeois ideology": "I ask the pardon of those teachers who, in dreadful conditions, attempt to turn the few weapons they can find in the history and learning to 'teach' against the ideology, the system and practices in which they are trapped. They are a kind of hero" (157). In Althusser's picture, educators face bleak prospects for meaningful resistance. They have "few weapons" and are "trapped" within the ideological system. Seemingly doomed to noble failure, these teachers are "a kind of hero."

This is an interesting, although brief, aside for Althusser. It is the only place in the entire article where he overtly mentions the potential for resistance. This resistance comes not from parents or students who feel some manifestation of (and thereby become conscious of) their own oppression. Instead it comes from teachers who "'teach' against the ideology" and, in so doing, attempt to teach others to see ideology at work. The teacher then plays a leadership role—albeit a limited one—in whatever attempts can be made to organize resistance; the very conditions that make schools the ideal place to inculcate the ideology of the ISA make them also the ideal place to teach others to be aware of it and so resist it, and the teacher is in the perfect position to take advantage of those conditions.

Althusser illustrates the structure of domination as a kind of inverted pyramid in terms that are strictly top-down. Such an illustration makes apparatuses of power visible, but this visibility is produced by means of monolithic terms that do not address the complexity of and possibility for the individual's role within this structure and within these apparatuses. As represented within the terms of Althusser's analysis (and for those such as Bowles and Gintis whose theories have been deeply influenced by his analysis), teacher and curriculum combine to make students internalize their positions within the capitalist mode of production and understand these positions as natural and right. For Althusser the individual subject is created by and through ideology, and this understanding is his greatest limitation because it fails to explain how participating in the structure is possible, how power works in productive as well as repressive ways, and how and why individuals find ways to resist and question their places. Yet others, too, find exploring docility easier than exploring resistance.

For Althusser as for Marx, the family obviously plays a key function in maintaining the class system. Annette Lareau's *Unequal Childhoods: Class, Race, and Family Life* allows us to see something of how class position is passed on from generation to generation. Her book offers case studies of twelve families (four middle class, four working class, and four in poverty); two families of each group were black and two were white. These case studies make visible the ways that child rearing itself is marked by class. "Concerted cultivation" is Lareau's term to describe middle-class assumptions about and practices of raising children:

> The white and black middle-class parents engaged in practices of *concerted cultivation*. In these families, parents actively fostered and assessed their children's talents, opinions, and skills. They scheduled their children for activities. They reasoned with them. They hovered over them and outside the home they did not hesitate to intervene on the children's behalf. They made a deliberate and sustained effort to stimulate children's development and to cultivate their cognitive and social skills. (238, author's italics)

Her term to describe working-class and poor parents' attitudes toward and practice of raising children is the "accomplishment of natural growth":

> The working-class and poor parents viewed children's development as unfolding spontaneously, as long as they were provided with comfort, food, shelter, and other basic support. . . . As with concerted cultivation, this commitment, too, required ongoing effort; sustaining children's natural growth despite formidable life challenges is properly viewed as accomplishment. Parents who relied on natural growth generally organized their children's lives so they spent time in and around home in informal play. . . . Boundaries between adults and children were clearly marked, parents generally used language not as an aim in itself but more as a conduit for social life. (238–39)

As in Shirley Brice Heath's seminal *Ways with Words: Language, Life, and Work in Communities and Classrooms* (discussed in chapter 3), Lareau found that the significant differences between the "cultural logics of child rearing" were not between black families and white families, but between middle-class families and working-class and poor families. Middle-class children, because of their parents' emphasis on language and negotiation and on learning and organized activities among nonfamily members, are better prepared for college and for middle-class employment opportunities. Working-class and poor children, however, tend to have stronger ties with their siblings and extended families and are better able to occupy themselves and take responsibility for their own entertainment. Also like Heath, interestingly, Lareau seems to find herself less drawn to the middle-class parents and children as middle-class life becomes "increasingly rationalized" (246).

Yet Lareau is careful to point out that working-class and poor children do not necessarily grow up to be working class or poor themselves. (In her description of one middle-class, dual career family, Lareau mentions that the parents are helping to support their parents and siblings still living in poverty.) Lareau writes, "To be sure, there are also significant amounts of upward and downward mobility. There are those in the population who overcome the predicted odds, particularly certain immigrant groups. The social structure of inequality is not all determining" (256). Early in the book, she states, "Perhaps two-thirds of the members of society ultimately reproduce their parents' level of educational attainment, while about one-third take a different path" (8). I wish to turn my attention to this one-third. Althusser and Lareau, from radically different perspectives, show how the individual is interpellated by and within culture. Yet, as Lareau also states (but does not demonstrate in her case studies), the individual has the potential to resist that interpellation. "The social structure of inequality" is not the result of an overt system of repression.

Antonio Gramsci, for example, specifically addresses the potential for the importance of teachers and education in any kind of organized resistance to repression. In his *Selections from the Prison Notebooks*, he describes the "new type of intellectual" whose position is marked by "active participation in practical life, as constructor, organizer, 'permanent persuader'" (11). Gramsci also develops the category of the "organic intellectual" who rises from the working class or from poverty to represent his own class and argues that "it is the organic intellectual who can speak most powerfully and persuasively for and from his class" (10). "School," writes Gramsci, "is the instrument through which intellectuals of various levels are elaborated" (10), and the teacher, by reason of her education and her participation in the production of knowledge, becomes a potentially potent agent of change for her students, as has been true for many who have been moved to mention their teachers in their published literacy narratives. Of course, we also know that teachers, unfortunately, have the potential to have the opposite effect.

But Gramsci and Lareau help us begin to see how power works in much more complex ways than Althusser describes. As with Althusser and Gramsci, Michel Foucault has been useful for contemporary critiques of higher education. Foucault, writing at the same time as Althusser, defines power as beyond the distinctions of class and race and refuses to consider it as top-down movement. For Foucault, no power vacuum, no neutral space, no "free zone" exists where the web of power is not stretched, and everyone, including teachers and students, is situated within that web. Foucault hypothesizes in "Power and Strategies" that "power is co-extensive with the social body; there are no spaces of primal liberty between the meshes of its network" (142). At the same time:

> one should not assume a massive and primal condition of domination, a binary structure with "dominators" on one side and "dominated" on the other, but rather a multiform production of relations of domination which are partially susceptible of integration into overall strategies. (142)

Power is always everywhere and is much too complex a concept to describe in binary terms of a downward movement from those-who-have-power to those-who-are-powerless, as Althusser does. Power is "multiform" (as opposed to uniform) and produced from "relations of domination" that in turn can be integrated into "strategies" that are productive. As Foucault explains in "Truth and Power":

> If power were never anything but repressive, if it never did anything but to say no, do you really think one would be brought to obey it? What makes power hold good, what makes it accepted, is simply the fact that it doesn't only weigh on us as a force that says no, but that it traverses and produces things, it induces pleasure, forms knowledge, produces discourse. It needs to be considered as a productive network which runs through the whole social body, much more than as a negative instance whose function is repression. (119)

Power cannot be contained by or limited to binary oppositions; neither is it to be thought of as "evil" or as bad in and of itself. It produces pleasure, knowledge, and things. Structures and strategies of power make learning in systematic ways and passing on that learning in systematic ways possible; structures and strategies of power not only make possible "our" standard of living, but also make any standard of living possible, such as in the ways we live work, and play. Of course, this is not to say that structures and strategies of power do not produce pain, real pain. And this is not to say that everyone is or should be happy wherever and however they are situated in their social, economic, political positions and relations at home, at work, and elsewhere. Obviously, there are people who are suffering and who fight to end that suffering as well as people who see and fight to end the suffering of others. But the subject is not so much trapped in the web of power as a participant in the play of power. Furthermore, resistance is a production of power's network, and paradigms can and do shift.

One of my favorite photographs of my daughter as a baby shows her on the floor, crawling on top of and thoroughly investigating my ancient copy of Ribner and Kittredge's *The Complete Works of Shakespeare*. The photograph serves as a visual metaphor for her relationship with literacy throughout her life thus far. She was immersed in literacy long before she had a say or a choice because my husband and I read to her with religious-like fervor almost from the very day we brought her home from the hospital. And she saw us, as students and as teachers, reading constantly. Now she's a young adult who remains an avid reader with a passion for ideas. In terms of the research, her literacy was predictable. But in terms of the same research, my literacy was not. Therefore, one goal of this book is to make sense of my own seemingly anomalous experience. More importantly, however, as a teacher, I want to believe that the desire for higher literacy is teachable, but in order to teach it, I need to have a better understanding of from where that desire comes.

Perhaps power is what motivates the desire for higher literacy, a desire that has fueled countless individual paradigm shifts. Certainly, power and desire are intimately entwined. But, as with Foucault, I am not thinking of power in an overt political or monetary sense. Nor am I describing a desire to be middle class, to have a "nice" house with "nice" things. For many, the desire for higher literacy has no connection with a desire to "rise" to another class status. Consider Harvey Pekar, for instance, creator of *American Splendor: The Life and Times of Harvey Pekar*, a "comic" book series that is smart and ironic but rarely comic. He lives in what many would see as squalor, surrounded by books and records, and he is an exceedingly well-read autodidact who has no desire to be viewed as middle class. And, for many, the desire for higher literacy functions to obscure class consciousness. So I define this desire, at this point, in the sense of wanting and feeling some measure of control over one's environment and some measure of control over one's place in that environment.

This project seeks to expand what teachers know about their students' as well as their own reading and writing to enable them to see in more complex ways what impedes or motivates their students' acquisition of higher literacy. I want to learn more about what turns so many students off from reading and writing as they work their ways through high school and college. I want to know more of what worked for the students who make it to college ready to tackle the more demanding literacy we require of them. I am particularly interested in the stories students from nonmainstream backgrounds tell because the scholarship in my field and my own experience as a teacher of composition (with more than seven years as a teacher of basic writing in addition to eleven years as a teacher of "regular" first-year writing courses) shows me that these students are the ones who struggle most painfully in the process of acquiring higher literacy.

The following chapters examine definitions and studies of the relationship between literacy and class and then explore literacy narratives to see how others from various class backgrounds characterize their desire for higher literacy. The next chapter focuses on these descriptions of individuals' relationships to literacy not to take them at face value or to view them as individual stories of success or failure, but to read their experiences and their representations of their desire for literacy as part of a larger cultural narrative of literacy education.

Chapter Two

Boundaries and Memories

Literacy Narrative as Genre

Tie into article.

Wɪᴛʜ ᴀ ʙʀᴀɴᴅ ɴᴇᴡ Pʜ.D., two years on the job market, and at the "advanced" age of forty-one, I called my mother with the news that I had finally been hired on the tenure track as an assistant professor. Her response? "You spent this many years in school and you're going to be someone's assistant?"

I begin this chapter with a brief personal story for a few reasons. For one thing, I hope it grabs the reader's attention. For another, it enables a kind of shorthand to pack a lot about who I am in a very brief space. Stories help establish our ethos as writers. They also (may) help explain difference to others. I have colleagues who cannot begin to imagine the attitudes toward education and work in my family. And, of course, the story allows me to show off—as if to say, see how far I have come and how much harder I have had to work than my colleagues who have families who supported their higher education.

H. Porter Abbott tells us:

wherever we look in this world, we seek to grasp what we see not just in space but in time as well. Narrative gives us this understanding; it gives us what could be called the shape of time. Accordingly, our narrative perception stands ready to be activated in order to give us a frame or context for even the most static and uneventful scenes. And without understanding the narrative, we often feel we don't understand what we see. We cannot find the meaning. Meaning and narrative understanding are very closely connected. . . . (11)

Framing an event or series of events as a story enables us to make sense of that event. I can remember desperately trying to narratize my chemistry chapters as I studied for tests. How could I tell myself a story about Boyle's Law to remember it? Perhaps if I had had more background information, I could have, but, suffice to say, I celebrated when I received a *C* as my final grade as a result of shameless groveling for extra credit.

Actually, the "groveling" part of the previous sentence is a lie I added to make the anecdote, or story, better. I do not recall ever having groveled to teachers because teacher's pets (women and men alike) were frequently physically threatened in my neighborhood and I never believed groveling would have any positive effect. I added that touch because embellishing, adding tiny details that do not change the outcome—a *C* in the class—but make the story somehow more real, more worth reading—the "supplementary events"—is so tempting. As Abbott explains, "The question concerning when retellings of a story like Cinderella can no longer claim the name of Cinderella leads us to another, broader issue: that of the relative importance of the events in a story" (20). Drawing from the work of Roland Barthes and Seymour Chatman, Abbott discusses the differences between "constituent" and "supplementary" events. Constituent events "are necessary for the story to be the story that it is. They are the turning points, the events that drive the story forward and that lead to other events" (20). The constituent events of my story are that I took a chemistry class, I struggled to find ways to make it make sense, and I earned a *C*. The "supplementary" events, on the other hand, "are not necessary for the story" and "can be removed and the story will still be recognizably the story that it is" (20). So the constituent events are the story's skeleton, and the supplementary events are the flesh and fashion. As Abbott puts it, "In short, there is more to narrative than story. And in that 'more' can be much that gives a work its power and significance" (20). The constituent events may draw us to a story in the first place, but the supplementary events keep us reading.

Much of Jerome Bruner's work concerns the human need for narrative, and he maintains that we use narrative to structure how we make sense of the world and of our place in it. In *The Culture of Education* he writes:

> There appear to be two broad ways in which human beings organize and manage their knowledge of the world, indeed structure their immediate experience: one seems more specialized for treating of physical "things," the other for treating of people and their plights. These are conventionally known as *logical-scientific* thinking and *narrative* thinking. . . . They have varied modes of expression in different cultures, which also cultivate them differently. No culture is without both of them, though different cultures privilege them differently." (39–40)

According to Bruner, then, narrative is basic to our being human. The need to understand our world via stories is hardwired into us, or, as Bruner states it, has its "roots in the human genome" or is a "given in the nature of language" (39). Narrative and culture are inextricably linked; without narrative, we have no culture. But narratives are crafted and told differently and serve different functions in different cultures.

So what produces these differences? What factors color our understanding of what makes a story worthy of being told? In other words, what can motivate a working-class "nobody" to tell his or her story—indeed, what makes a "nobody" think that he or she has a story to tell in the first place? We assume without question that the stories of kings or generals are worth telling, but what about the story of the commoner who has no starring role, historically speaking? In *Missing Persons: The Impossibility of Auto/Biography*, Mary Evans speculates that the Protestant Reformation figures in democratizing autobiography and leaves a space for telling one's story that was once filled by the act of confession:

> What has come to hold sway as a major "world vision" is thus the sense of accountability, of the need for explanation and documentation which are the inevitable results of Calvinism and Protestantism, and which, of course, provide such a fertile breeding-ground for the idea and development of auto/biography. Deprived of the religious means of literal confession and explanation, the impulse to confess, and to explain oneself (or others) is compelled and channeled into other sources." (15)

Once, we could tell our stories to our priests, and we could gauge the worthiness (or shock value) of our story by the response—sympathy or severe penance. Without confession, however, where do we turn with our stories? Evans points out that the rise of Protestantism in Europe coincided with the Enlightenment's growing valorization of individual worth that in turn nurtured rising capitalism and rising literacy rates: "Thus, at the same time as people (particularly in northern Europe) were becoming more literate and better educated, and cognizant of a more secular, and indeed rational, culture, they were removed from the emotional resource of sharing a sense of responsibility for faults and misdemeanors with those who could help them" (15). Evans sees a connection between the need for this "emotional resource" and the "tell-all auto/biography." "Marginalized by the accounts of the powerful, [individuals who cannot control the conventional organization of auto/biography] have little recourse (other than silence) except through disclosure" (15). Kings are remarkable by virtue of having been born kings; the rest of us must reveal something unexpected, and therefore, remarkable. To use Abbott's term, we must "supplement" the story of our existence.

Seeking "to understand the popularity of auto/biography with the book-buying public and the enthusiasm of authors for writing it," Evans argues that "what auto/biography does is to offer us a chance to stabilise the uncertainties of existence" (131). By "uncertainties of existence," she is referring to the fact that our standard of living appears to be stable, but we have to admit when pressed that our material lives can change rapidly and radically. Evans offers the example of twentieth-century Europe experiencing two world wars and the Holocaust. She writes, "We cannot tolerate the ambiguity of human existence, and we thus provide ourselves with icons of experience and reality" (143). Our efforts to shape our lives as coherent stories, stories that represent cultural shifts and boundaries, are as much acts of fiction as of nonfiction. Evans uses the slash in her spelling of *auto/biography* to emphasize that autobiography is just as much a construction of the real as the biography. Autobiography has no special purchase on truth. Evans, furthermore, argues that the "individual" is valorized over the social at the expense of the social:

> Recognition of the shared frailty of human experience and human existence is largely out of step with the grandiose expectations of the late twentieth-century West. Since we cannot accept this collective experience, we are forced to construct ever more complex individuals to reassure ourselves of our individuality. In feeding our culture's desire for managed difference, auto/biography helps us to turn our backs on the shared circumstances of social life. (143)

Here, at the conclusion of Evans's book, she claims that we are in denial regarding our vulnerability to catastrophe (especially human-made catastrophes such as war), and so we are drawn to narratives by individuals who have overcome great obstacles as we vicariously experience their triumph over adversity.

In a certain sense, we could say that such narratives serve the same purpose as Horatio Alger's late nineteenth-century fiction, which stressed the importance of the main character's "pluck and wit," as well as the ability to take advantage of opportunities when they became available. (Interestingly, Alger's heroes never raised themselves by their own bootstraps strictly speaking, but were always in the right place at the right time—and literate in the right ways. For example, in *Ragged Dick*, the protagonist saves a wealthy man's son from drowning and because he has worked diligently to learn to read, write, and cipher, he is ready to seize the opportunities made available by the grateful father.) Although we assume the nineteenth-century reader identified with Ragged Dick and his rise, we also know that for every Dick whose financial and social conditions improved, the conditions of countless others did not. So Dick serves not only as an outlet, but also as a vent. Evans's phrase "managed difference" emphasizes that difference is constructed along with the individual. Complexity is reserved for the individual whose ways of being different are reassuring rather than frightening or making no sense. The homeless schizophrenic's narrative can be told only once she has a home and her schizophrenia is responding to medication; a schizophrenic's narrative of schizophrenia cannot be "managed." Complexity is not what we wish to see when we look to "the shared circumstances of social life." There, we desire simplicity: work hard and you will be rewarded, education equals opportunity, and so forth.

Of course, I do not wish to make "managed difference" sound like a conspiracy theory citing a powerful "them" seeking to keep "us" under their powerful collective thumb. This process is not the product of conspiracy; it is how culture works. And the concept of the individual as constructed is certainly not exclusive to Evans's economic materialist worldview. Diane Bjorkland in *Interpreting the Self: Two Hundred Years of American Autobiography* draws from the work of sociologist George Mead when she writes, "The self . . . arises not only out of the interaction process with specific others but also by using ideas available for constructing a viewpoint of the self. Selves are culturally as well as socially constructed" (7). Consider, for example, the difficulty the general population has comprehending (much less discussing) transgendered individuals. Some time ago on her show, Oprah Winfrey's guest was Jennifer Boylan, a professor at Colby College, who was discussing her book *She's Not There: A Life in Two Genders*. Boylan was born a man but always felt she was a woman and finally reached a point where she could no longer continue to be a man. She has now changed genders but continues to live with her wife and two children. Winfrey's audience struggled to make sense of this "self" who did not fit any of their " ideas available for constructing a viewpoint of the self," and Winfrey herself worked patiently to help her audience through that struggle at the same time that Boylan worked to explain to everyone the evolution of her "real" self from male to female. Interestingly, Boylan's female self is easily identifiable and describable as she appeared on television in a conservative skirt and twin set. In other words, Boylan did not invent a new gender with a radically imagined mode of dress; she desired and took on a way of dress and being that is typically "feminine"—matronly, but feminine. What I find even more interesting—and not surprising—is that Boylan's wife refused to be interviewed. Her role, who she is, is now much more difficult to name and describe; we have no narrative from which to draw and here truly is the "self" who does not fit into the "ideas available for constructing a viewpoint of the self."

Bjorkland quotes Mead saying, "The human self arises through its ability to take the attitude of the group to which he belongs—because he can talk to himself in terms of the community to which he belongs"; however, she adds "that persons can also talk of themselves for this reason. Moreover, such self-conceptions are mediated by a language that is public and not private" (7–8; author's italics). In her interview with Winfrey, Boylan talked about her early sense of not being like other boys, in not feeling right in her own skin, yet she can only describe these sensations in the language available to her, the language that only allows for *he's* or *she's*. To make her experience comprehensible both to herself and to Winfrey's audience (as well as to the potential audience for the book she was publicizing on Winfrey's show), she must shape it into a story. As Bruner states, "It seems evident, then, that skill in narrative construction and narrative understanding is crucial to constructing our lives and a 'place' for ourselves in the possible world we will encounter" (40).

In addition, Bruner tells us that our skill at narration does not come into play just to explain the odd moments or anomalies in our lives, but that our skill at narration enables us to see our entire lives as part of one big story. I tell my students, as I work to help them make connections with what they read and write in class, that they are the stars of their own stories, so they can imagine how their stories will or will not intersect with what we read and write, and they can use what we read to help them expand and develop the narration of their own stories. As Bruner puts it:

> Life is not just one self-sufficient story after another, each narratively on its own bottom. Plot, characters, and setting all seem to continue to expand. We attempt to stabilize our worlds with an enduring pantheon of gods who continue to act in character, though circumstances change. We construct a "life" by creating an identity-conserving Self who wakes up the next day still mostly the same. We seem to be geniuses at the "continued story." (143–44)

If we are "geniuses" at seeing our lives as a long integrated and coherent story, that so many choose to write those stories down is not surprising, then. And as we are encouraged from every direction to see ourselves as unique and special individuals (even the U.S. Army exhorts us to "be all that [we] can be"), that more of us want to want to write our stories and explain and display our unique individuality to others is also not surprising.

Of course, our desire to represent ourselves in our "unique individuality" has itself garnered critical attention in past decades. In *Reading Autobiography: A Guide for Interpreting Life Narratives*, Sidonie Smith and Julia Watson write, "While autobiography is the most widely used and most generally misunderstood term for life narrative, it is also a term that has been rigorously challenged in the wake of postmodern and postcolonial critiques of the Enlightenment subject" (3). In a scholarly world that has read Derrida and Lacan, what are we to make of a genre that "celebrates the autonomous individual and the universalizing life story" (3)? What does it mean that so many of us feel the need—and act on that need—to tell our stories to others, to confess, if you will? For many, the motivation most likely comes from not seeing their experiences reflected in what they read and see. According to Smith and Watson:

This contemporary fascination with life narratives derives in part from the power of an ideology of individualism and its cultural hold on us. . . . We are also witnessing, in an outpouring of memories, the desire of autobiographical subjects to splinter monolithic categories that have culturally identified them, such as "woman" or "gay" or "black" or "disabled," and to reassemble various pieces of memory, experience, identity, embodiment, and agency into new, often hybrid, modes of subjectivity. In this pursuit, life narrative has proved remarkably flexible in adapting to new voices and assuming new shapes across media, ideologies, and the differences of subjects. (109)

So contained within the desire of writers of narratives to represent themselves rather than to be represented is also the desire to further "individuate" themselves by "splinter[ing] monolithic categories that have culturally identified them." In other words, not only is my experience as a female academic from a working-class background different from that of a male academic from a middle-class background, but it is also different from the experiences of other female academics from working-class backgrounds.

As our awareness of and sensitivity to difference and its multiple manifestations have increased, we find that we must complicate our ways of talking about narratives. Of the many literacy narratives I have read in researching this project, I have encountered the story of a mother who wrote advertising jingles in the 1950s to keep her large Irish Catholic family financially afloat, an African-American writer who credits the U.S. Air Force with making her escape from a bleak life in East St. Louis possible, a white writer whose elite literacy background includes anecdotes of her family competing with each other to answer GE College Bowl questions first, a white academic from a working-class family who identifies herself, a child of a communist, as a "red diaper baby," to cite but a few. As Laura Marcus writes:

Autobiographical theory now has to address itself to much more complex models of ethnic, gender, sexual and class identities. . . . This also raises problems of stereotyping by categorization and what Trinh T. Minh Ha has called "planned authenticity," in which a group may be required to accentuate its difference as defined by a dominant culture. From these perspectives, the battles between humanists and deconstructionists over the ideal subject appear irrelevant compared to the theoretical innovations and the changes in cultural awareness required to accommodate all these real writing subjects. (223)

In the literacy narrative, the writer's acquisition of increasingly complex forms of literacy figures prominently in how that writer understands his or her life. I am particularly interested in narratives individuals who come from poverty or working-class backgrounds, regardless of race, write because these often have the most to teach teachers about our students' and our own relationships to literacy. What motivates the writers of these narratives to become more highly literate? How do they describe their desire for that literacy? The remainder of this chapter asks these questions of quintessential literacy narratives. Frederick Douglass's narrative is truly a benchmark text that provides a standard with which to define the genre. Mike Rose's *Lives on the Boundary* has become commonplace in composition classes and composition scholarship. I include Richard Rodriguez's *Hunger of Memory: An Autobiography*, because his story is quickly recognizable to anyone who has taught composition for any length of time and because his narrative problematizes the genre and offers a case in point to support Min Zhan Lu's critique of Mina Shaughnessy (discussed later).

The thrust of the literacy narrative is how literacy—usually characterized as a love of fiction—changes the writer's life. In *Literacy and Literacies: Texts, Power, and Identity*, James Collins and Richard Blot use the phrase "literate salvation" to describe the way literacy figures as a key to the writer's success in life. Certainly writers from elite backgrounds focus on their love for reading and the special place books hold in their lives. For example, Anne Fadiman's *Ex Libris: Confessions of a Common Reader* describes her lifelong passion for books in the context of her family's legacy of their lifelong passion for books. Fadiman is the daughter of Clifton Fadiman, one of the most prominent proselytizers for higher literacy, who was actively involved in the Book-of-the-Month Club, edited collections of children's literature, and made encouraging literacy for everyone his life's work. But many times, when the writer of the literacy narrative comes from poverty or a working-class background, literacy is represented as a life saver. This is not to say that race does not figure importantly; however, as Shirley Brice Heath's and Annette Lareau's research shows, class trumps race in many ways. Both *Ways with Words* and *Unequal Childhoods* show how middle-class whites and blacks have more in common with each other than do middle-class blacks and working-class blacks. As Heath states:

> A natural tendency of readers of this book will be to highlight the different racial memberships of Trackton and Roadville. Some readers will want to explain the differences between the attitudes, events, and patterns of communication of the two communities in terms of race only, overlooking the fact that the blacks and whites who were the townspeople [that is, middle class] had far more in common with each other than with either Roadville or Trackton (10).

In the discussion that follows, while I certainly will not ignore race or pretend our society is colorblind—certainly race figures prominently—I will focus much more specifically on class and the common tropes that emerge and reemerge in working-class literacy narratives.

On the surface, Frederick Douglass's telling and retelling of his transformation from slave to freeman to public intellectual overtly identifies literacy as the prime force in that transformation. The bare bones of Douglass's story—the constituent events in Abbott's terms—are that he learned to read, escaped slavery, and went on to become a powerful antislavery spokesman. The supplementary events, on the other hand, dramatize the dangers involved in all his undertakings and, most important, the ways he used his literacy to establish his humanity and authority. Douglass was so certain of the importance of his story that he wrote and published three versions. He wrote the first in 1845 largely to answer charges from doubting audiences that he had never been a slave. His 1881 *Life and Times of Frederick Douglass* not only updated his life story and kept his name and reputation alive, but in it he also attempted to keep the aftermath of slavery and the plight of African Americans in the public consciousness during late Reconstruction when white Americans were all too willing to put both behind them. All three narratives establish and maintain Douglass's credentials as one worthy to speak and be heard.

Each narrative tells the story of Douglass's learning to read and write, his growing consciousness of literacy's power, and his continuing efforts to speak and write against slavery. Literacy is integral to each representation. He is for many reasons a fascinating and compelling figure. A man of driving ambition, Douglass, in his literary representations of himself as liberated slave, both makes use of and resists Northern culture to create a working position from which to be heard as a political activist and intellectual. Literacy and liberation are inextricably tied for Douglass, the one inevitably leading to the other as he took care to illustrate in each of his three autobiographies. In each version, for example, he narrates his revelation as to literacy's power to "forever unfit him to be a slave" after his master Hugh Auld forbids his learning to read (*Frederick Douglass* 47). Also in each he tells a story of his reading in *The Columbian Orator* of an encounter between a master and his thrice-escaped slave. In the story the slave is able, through the power of his rhetoric, to convince the master to free him. This story becomes emblematic of literacy's power to persuade, and Douglass strives throughout his life to achieve and maintain that power.

Contemporary critics point to the importance and influence of Douglass's argument regarding literacy's causal relationship to freedom. Valerie Smith in *Self-Discovery and Authority in Afro-American Narrative*, for example, identifies the 1845 work as "the point of departure for numerous critical studies of Afro-American literature." She continues, "If Douglass's *Narrative* is the referent to which dozens of later black narratives look back, then the cluster of scenes in which his autobiographical persona learns to read is the one which is most frequently echoed. . . . Moreover, when he links the acquisition of literacy to the process of liberation, he forges a connection that resonates for subsequent generations of writers" (1–2). Similarly, in *Literacy and Literacies: Texts, Power, and*

Identity, Collins and Blot write, "In Douglass's life and career, we find an early, defining example of the trope of literacy and liberation—of the perceived link between literacy, freedom, and financial independence. The liberationist motif captures a powerful historical impulse, whatever the complex realities" (80). What becomes generally understood to be the universal signifier of humanity in the nineteenth century is the human ability to use language; therefore, writing his story becomes the public performance of Douglass's humanity.

As Douglass represents it in his autobiographies, the narrative of liberation is intimately tied with the narrative of literacy. Literacy, according to all three narratives, automatically produces the desire for liberation. As Abbott writes, "Desire, wedded to the suggestiveness of narrative succession, is an awfully powerful combination" (39). We want to see a clear connect between literacy and liberation because the seeming logic appears unimpeachable. The more we know, the smarter we are; the smarter we are, the more we should desire the freedom to know more in a progressive, dialectical cycle. Abbott continues, stating that:

> it isn't just our human desire, plus illusion, that makes us suckers for this logic. We fall for it in part because so often during our lives we have actually experienced stories (true ones) in which *post hoc ergo propter hoc* seems to be vividly confirmed. . . . So there is a good empirical basis to explain why, when reading narratives, we should be tempted to apply this paradigm more quickly than we ought to. The error lies in passing from the valid assumption that all effects follow their causes to the false one that to follow something is to be an effect of that thing. A cause can in fact be any number of things, or any combination of things, that precede an effect, not necessarily the thing the narrative draws to our attention. (39–40)

In Douglass's narration, the epiphanal moment of his realization of literacy's power comes in response to Auld's passionate chastisement of his wife when she wants to teach Douglass to read the Bible. But, of course, Douglass's precociousness was most likely what initially made the Aulds decide to bring him to Baltimore to serve as their son's servant and companion. Representing his moment of revelation as an ironic result of his owner's efforts to produce the opposite effect serves Douglass's rhetorical purpose. And it makes a great story. In his seminal essay "Life as Narrative," Jerome Bruner writes:

> [E]ventually the culturally shaped cognitive and linguistic processes that guide the self-telling of life narratives achieve the power to structure perceptual experience, to organize memory, to segment and purpose-build the very "events" of a life. In the end, we become the autobiographical narratives by which we "tell about" our lives. And given the cultural shaping to which I referred, we also become variants of the culture's canonical forms. (694)

In other words, if we tell a story often enough, embellishing and adding details to make it a better story, it becomes real—whether it is "really" real or not. Certainly, Douglass, more than most, having written three versions of his life narrative—each significantly longer than the one before, can be said to have "become the autobiographical narrative." And our reading of these three narratives further cements our assumptions regarding literacy's cause-and-effect relationship to liberation.

What, then, does his story have to teach us about teaching? What I read in Douglass's narratives is that his education came largely through the knowledge of the importance of his own story combined with the practices of telling and retelling and the writing and rewriting of that story in his autobiographies. In the narratives of his own learning and literacy acquisition, Douglass challenged "standards" about what freed slaves did and did not know, how they did and did not learn, what they were and were not able to do. He offers the same challenge to contemporary teachers working with contemporary "nontraditional" students. Given the complex nature of knowledge and how it is defined, what would it take to teach in such a way that students were certain of the importance of their stories and that their telling and retelling of those stories would enable them to speak and write from positions of authority?

One contemporary educator takes up this challenge—another "representative" man who uses his own literacy narrative to establish his authority to speak and write. Mike Rose's *Lives on the Boundary* is a combination literacy narrative and critique of contemporary literacy education. His own experience as a child of poor parents and as an indifferent student who found his way academically with the help of caring teachers positions him to view the classroom through the eyes of both teacher and nontraditional student. His book begins:

> This is a hopeful book about those who fail. *Lives on the Boundary* concerns language and human connection, literacy and culture, and it focuses on those who have trouble reading and writing in the schools and the workplace. It is a book about the abilities hidden by class and cultural barriers. And it is a book about movement: about what happens as people who have failed begin to participate in the educational system that has seemed so harsh and distant to them. (ix)

Mike Rose is a believer in the potential of students, teachers, and schools to succeed. Despite the sad stories of failure that surround us, Rose remains "hopeful" (ix). Obviously, then, *Lives on the Boundary* is much more than just Rose's story, a story that could be reduced to a formula along the lines of working-class white guy becomes highly educated and makes good as a teacher and writer. But Rose's book takes on big ideas and dramatically challenges assumptions about remediation and who "belongs" in college. As Candace Spigelman, writing about Rose and others, states, "By embedding [his] personal stories into contexts in which race, class, and gender and other constructs are made visible, [Rose] seek[s] to subvert traditional political and cultural associations relating to personal achievement" (65). Nowhere does Rose employ the trope of the "self-made" man; in fact, he goes out of his way to insist that his is a case of "there but for fortune." He does not allow us to dismiss failure as being the student's "fault." Instead, he forces us, via story after story from his experience as a student and then as a teacher, to see the cultural forces at work in failure. Rose clearly demonstrates that damage can be done in the name of education at the same time that he offers his own story of ultimate success.

Collins and Blot point out that the book's "very title, with its 'boundary,' evokes the acts of inclusion and exclusion." They go on to describe *Lives on the Boundary* as "a hybrid work, part educational memoir, part teacher's story, part extended essay on the challenges facing American education" (109). In *Lives on the Boundary*, Rose tells the story of his academic life, from underprepared child in a struggling working-class family to a teacher of other underprepared students on both the elementary and the college levels. Rose argues throughout his book that educators' and pundits' jeremiads over our educational system's collapse ignore the fact that we are trying to educate absolutely everyone with no exceptions and that ours is "a system attempting to honor—through wrenching change—the many demands of a pluralistic society" (7). It is important that he tell his story because his story establishes his credentials to represent both his experience as well as the experiences of others. But the verb *to represent* is mine, not his. In fact, he resists the word: "Representative men are often overblown characters; they end up distorting their own lives and reducing the complexity of the lives they claim to represent" (8–9). Throughout his book, he scrupulously works to open windows on the complicated lives students from poverty and the working class face as they try to balance education with family and work and try to negotiate the vagaries of changing or erratic work schedules, public transportation, illnesses—all the complicating factors that undermine their educational ambitions. Rose sees and draws many connections between his and his students' struggles with literacy.

Rose grew up in a declining, working-class neighborhood in Los Angeles. His father's health was poor, and his mother worked as a waitress to support the family. As in all literacy narratives, he discovered reading and began reading voraciously. He was not a straight-*A* student, so being placed in the vocational track did not seem out of the ordinary. If a science teacher had not gone out of his way to check Rose's placement, he would most likely have remained in vocational classes. His mother, like mine, probably would never have questioned the school's authority. At an all-male Catholic high school, Rose attracted the notice and came under the important influence of Jack McFarland, his English teacher and mentor. Through McFarland, a truly extraordinary and exceptionally caring teacher, he discovered literature, film, and ideas, and he began to think of himself as an intellectual; also through McFarland, he found himself attending college where still more caring teachers intervened to keep him from floundering and flunking out and worked to make sure he received a real education, that he did not just go through the motions or slide through. (One teacher even devised a special series of courses to provide the cultural and theoretical background Rose needed to succeed.)

The transition from college to graduate school proved more difficult, and, perhaps because he found himself without the sponsors he needed, he left his graduate program and joined Teacher Corps, thus taking his education into another important direction. In Teacher Corps, Rose worked with at-risk students and model teachers and learned to take the time to learn where students come from and how where they come from can affect where they are academically. The next stage of his education/career took him to the University of California, Los Angeles (UCLA) and a special program for Vietnam-War veterans, a student group that further reinforced his understanding of students as complex individuals with fully realized lives as opposed to the characterizations of students as in need of "development" that emerged in basic writing scholarship of the 1970s and 1980s. UCLA and underprepared students then became his career focus. As he makes clear in his introduction, he offers his story because it resonates with the stories he has seen played out again and again in the lives of the students he has worked with, from grade school to college. His story opens a window for the rest of us to view something of these stories and these lives:

> the isolation of neighborhoods, information poverty, the limited means of protecting children from family disaster, the predominance of such disaster, the resilience of imagination, the intellectual curiosity and literate enticements that remain hidden from the schools, the feelings of scholastic inadequacy, the dislocations that come from crossing educational boundaries. (*Lives* 9)

His own literacy narrative provides the rhetorical backbone to stand up to critics who might charge him with romanticizing or sentimentalizing the stories he tells of his students' lives and schooling.

At this point, I wish to focus on three themes running through Rose's narrative: reading as "passport" or escape, the roles teachers can play, and the effects assumptions can have on students in our classrooms. "Escape" as a metaphor for the reader's relationship to reading occurs again and again in literacy narratives but perhaps especially in the literacy narratives written by those in poverty or from working-class backgrounds. Reading is the key that unlocks doors leading to ways of life other than the one being lived. Being engrossed in a book becomes a vital survival skill. Rose writes, for example, "I would check out my books two at a time and take them home to curl up with a blanket on my chaise longue, reading, sometimes, through the weekend, my back aching, my thoughts lost between galaxies. I became the hero of a thousand adventures, all with intricate plots and the triumph of good over evil, all many dimensions removed from the dim walls of the living room" (*Lives* 21). For countless working-class and poor children, reading becomes the means to other worlds and to consciousness of those other worlds. I still have the ability, much to the irritation of others at times, to become so utterly immersed in a book that I cannot hear anything around me. I do not know that this is an ability I consciously developed, but it served me well in bad times. As a child, I can remember feeling that my book world was much more "real" than my real world, and that it was preferable goes without saying. Rose also identifies reading as revealing social possibilities as well: "Reading opened up the world" (*Lives* 21) as he borrowed from and developed the stories he read into stories he told other kids: "[t]hese stories created for me a temporary community" (*Lives* 22). In other words, his reading served to help him escape being a nobody or, worse, a victim.

Collins and Blot, however, cite Rose's use of the metaphor of escape as problematic. They write:

> Escaping the boundaries of home and neighborhood becomes a persistent theme in Rose's account, but it contributes to a troubling inconsistency in *Lives*. Rose is relentlessly empathetic about the circumstances, efforts and failures of others. . . . Rose insightfully explores the logic underlying people's efforts and failures in schoolwork. He connects people's fears, hopes and literate aspirations to their homes and neighborhoods. (112)

A hallmark of Rose's scholarship is certainly his efforts to treat his students and their stories with respect, and another is his determination to find the logic in their reading and writing. Glynda Hull and Rose's Braddock Award–winning article "That Wooden Shack Place," for example, demonstrates the logic behind a student's seemingly aberrant reading of a poem. By means of an extended one-on-one discussion with the student, Rose is able to understand that the student's reasoning is perfectly accurate; the "problem" is that the student does not share the same cultural background as the poet or the teacher. I routinely assign the essay to help teaching assistants aspire to that level of ability to hear what our students have to say and understand how they are reading and interpreting their assigned texts.

But Collins and Blot criticize Rose for being "at once detailed and schematic" in his descriptions of his own life and relationship to education and for "polariz[ing] family and neighborhood versus the promise of education" (112). Pointing particularly to Rose's representation of his moving out of the trailer behind his mother's house after Lou Minton's suicide as liberating and his changing attitude toward school as "empowering," they argue, "It is

part of a familiar, if poignant, modern narrative, a tale of backwardness transformed, fetters broken, in the light-and-might of knowledge and schooling;
we should remain skeptical" (112–13). They continue by further arguing that
Rose's representation should be examined next to Heath's representation of
the "Townspeople" whose ways of using and valuing language are used and
valued in the schools, which has the effect of virtually ensuring their success over their working-class and poor classmates. Such a comparison would
reveal "a dramatic rendering of the apparent determination of class, literacy,
and identity" (113). In other words, Collins and Blot seem to be saying that
Rose fails to read his own background as empathetically as he does others'
and so falls into a trap of wedding the working class to a bleak picture of failure, decline, and dysfunction.

I can see Collins and Blot's argument, but I remain largely sympathetic to
Rose's representation. He is telling the story of his perception of his "escape"
from a life at "the culture's lost core" (*Lives* 46). Within this story—his story—
education indeed proved to be a passport to a different—better—way of life.
Rose is not arguing that school invariably offers the same passport to all. He
writes, "Some people who manage to write their way out of the working-class
describe the classroom as an oasis of possibility" (*Lives* 18). But he is careful
to show that he is not one of those people. Not until his junior year in high
school did he begin to see school in more positive, empowering terms, and his
teacher Jack McFarland was the catalyst for that change. Another key theme
of Rose's narrative is the power teachers have to make a difference in their
students' lives, and if Rose is vulnerable to a charge of romanticizing anywhere,
this is the place. Rose is an unapologetic advocate of teachers; to write his
book *Possible Lives*, he took a year to travel around the country to observe great
teaching on all levels, under all kinds of conditions and circumstances, so Rose,
more than most, goes out of his way to honor teachers and teaching.

He is unabashedly admiring in his introduction of this teacher who
made such a difference in his life: "Mr. McFarland had a master's degree
from Columbia and decided, at twenty-six, to find a little school and teach
his heart out" (*Lives* 32). McFarland is clearly a model for the teacher Rose
would become as he "brought a prep school model to Mercy High" (*Lives* 32),
"[made] potentially difficult book[s] accessible with his own explanations"
(*Lives* 33), and "immers[ed his students] in language" (*Lives* 33). McFarland
gathers a group of boys around him and offers them his own version of a salon,
and Rose quickly becomes addicted to books and ideas as McFarland, the
quintessential nerd in bad tie and wrinkled pants, begins to challenge these
boys to read, think, write, and discuss. According to Rose, McFarland is able
not only to keep order, but also to raise the bar for learning. "Tomfoolery, not
to mention assault, had no place in the world he was trying to create for us,
and instinctively everyone knew this" (*Lives* 33). Rose is at his most romantic

here as he describes student after student apparently swept up in McFarland's charismatic personality. Rose, of all people, knows how students will use strategies ranging from "tomfoolery" to assault to keep teachers at arm's length and to prevent everyone from learning, not just themselves. But McFarland is truly exceptional. (I cannot imagine any of my high school teachers inviting me or my fellow students to their homes or sharing books with us; I cannot even remember any of their names.)

Rose overtly refers to teaching as romance when he describes teaching at El Monte Elementary School for Teacher Corps. He writes:

> Teaching, I was coming to understand, was a kind of romance. You didn't just work with words or a chronicle of dates or facts about the suspension of protein in milk. You wooed kids with those things, invited a relationship of sorts, the terms of connection being the narrative, the historical event, the balance of casein and water. . . . Knowledge gained its meaning, at least initially, through a touch on the shoulder, through a conversation of the kind [my teachers] used to have with their students. My first enthusiasm about writing came because I wanted a teacher to like me. (*Lives* 102)

In other words, teaching is a kind of seduction; the personal relationship and the desire for a kind of intimacy provide fuel for the teacher to teach and the student to learn. And the teacher has the responsibility to initiate this relationship, to help students forge connections with the words or dates or facts, if not because they care about the words or dates or facts, then because they care about the teacher.

Jack McFarland is certainly this kind of teacher. He literally turns Rose's life around, pulling strings to get him into college and then helping him get a loan to pay for it. But more important, McFarland has enabled Rose to begin to think of himself as an intellectual, has served as his "sponsor," and has ushered him into a world of ideas. Deborah Brandt in her article "Sponsors of Literacy" argues that literacy is never acquired without some sort of "sponsorship":

> Sponsors, as I have come to think of them, are any agents, local or distant, concrete or abstract, who enable, support, teach, model, as well as recruit, regulate, suppress or withhold literacy—and gain advantage by it in some way. . . . Although the interests of the sponsored do not have to converge (and, in fact, may conflict), sponsors nevertheless set the terms for access to literacy and wield powerful incentives for compliance and loyalty. (166)

Sponsors, according to Brandt, can be parents, friends, bosses, or teachers, and they can sponsor in the positive ways we normally recognize and expect, that is, we expect parents and teachers to encourage literacy, or in negative ways we may not recognize as sponsorship, such as when we do something to prove to others who expressed doubt that we could, in fact, succeed.

Rose was exceedingly lucky in having several effective, positive sponsors; with Jack McFarland's help and foundation, he found more powerful sponsorship in teacher after teacher at Loyola Marymount University in Los Angeles. Rose writes that his teachers "collectively gave me the best sort of liberal education, the kind longed for in the stream of blue-ribbon reports on the humanities that now cross my desk. I developed the ability to read closely, to persevere in the face of uncertainty and ask questions of what I was reading—not with downcast eyes, but freely, aloud, realizing there is no such thing as an open book" (*Lives* 58). He describes their relationships to books and ideas as "alive" and states that "they lived their knowledge. And maybe because of that their knowledge grew in me in ways that led back out to the world. I was developing a set of tools with which to shape a life" (*Lives* 58). Here are the best sorts of sponsors, modeling a life of the mind balanced with family life and inviting others to share that life, and Rose, the working-class boy, was able to take advantage of this sponsoring and thrive.

Interestingly, however, he did not find graduate school so amenable. There, he found himself without that intensive sponsorship, and he floundered. He could find no reason to keep reading; the life of the mind no longer seemed "alive." As I train and mentor teaching assistants and teach graduate courses in my department, I can see students struggle with that same transition. Because my university, a second-tier research institution, tends to attract students from nontraditional backgrounds on all levels, I know that the students from the most nontraditional of backgrounds will need the most mentoring and support, and I know that class is a far greater determiner of who will most likely find themselves struggling than any other factor. Brandt writes, "When this process [of the pursuit of literacy] stirs ambivalence, on [our students'] part or on ours, we need to be understanding" ("Sponsors" 183). Ambivalence is not, then, an outlandish response to the pursuit of higher and higher literacy. Literacy, then, cannot merely serve as an escape; it also has to contribute to our senses of who we are and our senses that our literacy serves a purpose.

But what of the students who do not thrive, who never experience or appreciate the gift of a Jack McFarland? The third theme Rose pursues throughout his narrative is that "Students will float to the mark you set" (*Lives* 26). Mistakenly placed in vocational education, Rose assumes the placement is correct and simply "floats." Annette Lareau points out in *Unequal Childhoods*:

> working-class and poor parents often fear doing "the wrong thing" in school-related matters. They tend to be much more respectful of educators' professional expertise than are their middle-class counterparts. Thus, working-class and poor parents typically are deferential rather than demanding toward school personnel; they seek guidance from educators rather than giving advice to them; and they try to maintain a separation between school and home rather than foster an interconnectedness. (198)

The Pygmalion Effect.

Neither Rose nor his parents consider questioning what appears to them to be a result of careful judgment on the basis of "educators' professional expertise"; that the placement could be the result of a careless mistake never occurs to them. Yet Rose characteristically uses that experience in vocational education to extend further his empathy for and his knowledge of students on the boundaries of our various educational institutions. As a vocational education student, he can now see the ways he "dumbed down" without even realizing it; more important, he could see the slow process of being taught to reject education by the very institution entrusted with educating him, of learning to protect oneself from all that is implied by being placed in the vocational education track:

> If you're a working-class kid in the vocational track, the options you'll have to deal with this will be constrained in certain ways: You're defined by your school as "slow"; you're placed in a curriculum that isn't designed to liberate you, but to occupy you, or, if you're lucky, train you, though the training is for work the society does not esteem; other students are picking up the cues from your school and interacting with you in particular ways. (*Lives* 28)

In self-defense, students take on a tough persona that rejects the identity that the school thrusts upon them, and, thus, they end up rejecting everything associated with school—"books, essays, tests, academic scrambling, complexity, scientific reasoning, philosophical inquiry" (*Lives* 29). Rose opines, "The tragedy is that you have to twist the knife in your own gray matter to make this defense work" (*Lives* 29). Even more tragic is the great number of students who twist that knife.

Combined with this rejection of school identity can be a home identity that may not value "complexity, scientific reasoning, philosophical inquiry." Rose's parents encouraged him with chemistry sets and did not discourage or disparage his weekends spent reading. They wanted the best for him and so scraped together the money to send him to a Catholic school. Many working-class parents, however, perhaps themselves the products of vocational education, reinforce the rejection of school culture in the home. Lareau's study of poor and working-class as well as middle-class families found that "[r]ather than extensive negotiation, [working-class] parents use directives, and, when necessary, threats of physical punishment" (107). Inquiry was certainly never encouraged in my house when I was growing up; asking questions was often perceived as "talking back"; and efforts to negotiate were often met with "because I said so." In other words, few attractive models are available for the "working-class kid in the vocational track." As Collins and Blot point out, from his experience in vocational education, Rose "provides a first person account of Foucauldian power-knowledge: how a system of depersonalized measurement, normalized distribution, and consequent segregation has profound consequences for possible identities" (111). The "system," however, is hardly systematic and is even more frightening when we see that such measurement, distribution, and segregation can so easily take place by chance or mistake, and only chance again, in the form or another caring and interested teacher, places Rose in college preparatory courses—and leads him to Jack McFarland, the teacher we all wish we had known in school.

Rose is clearly aware that he had lucky breaks at key moments. One can contemplate the "what if's": What if his biology teacher had not bothered to question his placement in vocational education? What if he had never had a class with Jack McFarland? We want to believe that good students will succeed, but Rose, via his own story and his telling the stories of many of his students, forces us to see that a working-class student's rise happens with the help of a lot of sponsorship, and the odds are not in his or her favor. He writes:

> American meritocracy is validated and sustained by the deep-rooted belief in equal opportunity. But can we really say that kids like those I taught have equal access to America's educational resources? Consider not only the economic and political barriers they face, but the fact, too, that judgments about their ability are made at a very young age, and those judgments, accurate or not, affect the curriculum they receive, their place in the school, they way they're defined institutionally. (*Lives* 128)

Rose's varied experience from the personal to the professional reveals how the rhetoric of equality can serve to conceal the lack of opportunities for those students facing "economic and political barriers." His success was more the result of luck and supportive teachers than his own "pluck and wit." But he argues that we have the power to change so that the rhetoric more closely reflects the reality. To enact this change, he writes, "We'll need a pedagogy that encourages us to step back and consider the threat of the standard classroom and that shows us, having stepped back, how to step forward to invite a student across the boundaries of that powerful room" (*Lives* 238). Rose experienced such an invitation from Jack McFarland and from others, and he wants to reproduce that experience for others. Rose's representation of his life as he uses his education to make his way slowly out of the working class includes several rough spots and tough times, but one never doubts that Rose is thrilled to have "entered the conversation" that marks the best of what education can offer. Of course, not all of Rose's classmates responded to McFarland's invitation, and one reason Rose responded so passionately to McFarland's invitation might have been his bleak home life. In addition, some who respond to education's invitation do not view their transition as unproblematically as Rose does.

Richard Rodriguez's *Hunger of Memory: An Autobiography* has become a staple of writing courses—perhaps as a result of its figuring prominently in David Bartholomae and Anthony Petrosky's *Facts, Artifacts, and Counterfacts:*

Theory and Method for a Reading and Writing Course and *Ways of Reading*. Interestingly, as I did research to see how others have read Rodriguez's narrative, I found surprisingly little. A CompPile search, for example, turned up only seven hits—two were doctoral dissertations and the other five came from a 1982 issue of *Change*. As I checked the bibliographies of a dozen or so scholarly books in composition, virtually all references to *Hunger of Memory* were made in assignments and student writing.

Certainly Rodriguez's book, particularly his chapters "Aria" and "The Achievement of Desire," has become standard in composition and basic writing courses. In the introduction to *Ways of Reading*, Bartholomae and Petrosky provide a brief synopsis of "The Achievement of Desire," which reveals something of how and why it has proved so fruitful a text to assign first-year college students:

> Rodriguez tells the story of his education, of how he was drawn to imitate his teachers because of his desire to think and speak like them. His is not a simple story of hard work and success, however. In a sense, Rodriguez's education gave him what he wanted—status, knowledge, a way of understanding himself and his position in the world. At the same time, his education made it difficult to talk to his parents, to share their point of view; and to a degree, he felt himself becoming consumed by the powerful ways of seeing and understanding represented by his reading and his education. The essay can be seen as Rodriguez's attempt to weigh what he had gained against what he had lost. (2)

Here is Rodriguez's dilemma in a nutshell, and why so many writing teachers continue to bring Rodriguez into their classrooms is easy to see. The conflict he describes is what many students from nontraditional backgrounds face, but are unlikely to predict because little in their backgrounds prepares them to make such a prediction. The greater the difference between their backgrounds and college, the greater the conflict can be. Rodriguez, although he has more frequently than not been met with resistance by the students in my classes, can at least offer a glimpse of education's potential to separate them to some degree from their family and friends. However, even many teachers are blithely unaware of this conflict as they assume, much like Collins and Blot see Rose doing, that the appropriation of Standard American English and a move to the middle class can only be perceived as positive and desirable.

Unlike Rose, however, Rodriguez describes himself as "[a]n enchantedly happy child" (4). He continues, "Mine was a childhood of intense family closeness. And extreme public alienation" (4). Rodriguez cites education as that which "altered" his life and "carried [him] far" (5). He tells a complicated story of literacy in which language—specifically Spanish rather than English—serves to establish a binary between family (love, togetherness, warmth) and education (ambivalence, solitude, sterility). Of course, all of his siblings were educated and did not suffer the same anxiety (as far as we know), but he is the one who became highly literate; he is the one who craved literacy. Yet this intense desire comes later. At first, as he enters school, he sees language itself in binary terms: Spanish is private and related to family, whereas English is public and reserved for school. He writes, "Supporters of bilingual education today imply that students like me miss a good deal by not being taught in their family's language. What they seem not to recognize is that, as a socially disadvantaged child, I considered Spanish to be a private language. What I needed to learn in school was that I had the right—and the obligation—to speak the public language of *los gringos*" (19). He goes on to argue that a bilingual classroom may have made his entry into school somewhat less frightening, but it would have enabled him to put off "learning the great lesson of school, that I had a public identity" (19). So at the same time he longs for that lost sense of a closed, safe environment, he knows it had to be lost as he and his siblings grew older and increasingly connected to people outside that environment. Still, it saddens him that language has served to separate all of them from their parents to some extent: "The family's quiet was partly due to the fact that, as we children learned more and more English, we shared fewer and fewer words with our parents" (25). In a certain sense, his nostalgia is not unlike that longing for the time in many families' lives when the children are small and their world centers on their parents.

Yet Rodriguez's sense of separation is not merely a natural result of age as children become more peer-centered than family-centered. Not only does language separate him from his family, but increasingly literacy and his inexplicable "hunger" for books mark him as the odd one as well. As early as the third grade Rodriguez's intense desire for learning manifests itself: "with ever-increasing intensity, I devoted myself to my studies. I became bookish, puzzling to all my family. Ambition set me apart" (45). He cites no alluring, exciting invitations from a Jack McFarland, just nameless nuns who "made my success their ambition" (44). Instead, by way of explanation for his academic achievement, he writes, "What I am about to say to you has taken me more than twenty years to admit: *A primary reason for my success in the classroom was that I couldn't forget that schooling was changing me and separating me from the life I enjoyed before becoming a student*" (45, author's italics). At first reading, this admission makes little sense. Why would he desire that separation from his "enchanted childhood"? He does not (and most likely cannot) answer this question. His academic success allows him to measure the distance from his childhood and family; he transfers his allegiance from his family to his teachers.

In high school, he does not want to be a teacher as much as he "wanted to *be* like my teachers, to possess their knowledge, to assume their authority, their confidence, even to assume a teacher's persona" (55; author's italics). One can *wiring + environment*

ask again, where does this desire come from? What drives this identification? In *Reading Richard Rodriguez's Hunger of Memory*, Paul L. Rowe observes:

> One of the problems of the working-class academic is the genuine sense of ambivalence toward education. Education often does seem, especially initially, as a liberating force, freeing one from the repressions associated with working-class life. These can range from demeaning and deadening work to abusive home situations, sexism, homophobia, and anti-intellectualism. Middle-class teachers and fellow students can offer a liberalism and an understanding on these matters that can be refreshing and liberating. Education can help individuals remake themselves, can serve as a second parent or family or culture that is preferable in some ways to the first. (204)

At the same time, Rodriguez is aware that his education is separating him from his family, he is also aware that his teachers have a kind of understanding he will never have at home. Of course, his family situation is not "abusive," but certainly as he grows older, he can see his parents' lack of power outside the walls of their home, whereas his teachers, to a third grader's eyes, appear to be powerful and knowing, having the confidence his parents lack. Rodriguez's attraction to his teachers is largely an attraction to what he perceives as their power.

Rodriguez somewhat grimly lays out his childhood march to becoming the quintessential "scholarship boy." In the fourth grade, he demands reading suggestions from his teachers, making lists and checking off each completed book. In sixth grade, he is not content merely to read his listed books, but must include in his list a statement of each book's starkly stated and reduced theme; *Wuthering Heights* is summed up as a warning against "the danger of 'letting emotions get out of control'" (62). He observes that he "was not a good reader. Merely bookish, I lacked a point of view when I read. Rather, I read in order to acquire a point of view" (64). Neither does college offer relief to this picture unless we count his discovery of Richard Hoggart's metaphor of the "scholarship boy" from *The Uses of Literacy*. Here is his moment of epiphany as his reading of Hoggart enables him to make sense of his own experience: "Scholarship boy: good student, troubled son" (48). He realizes that the scholarship boy "cannot afford to admire his parents" because he is so single-mindedly working toward such a different way of life. (49). At no point in his memoir does Rodriguez ever describe reading as pleasurable as most writers of literacy narratives do. Rodriguez's representation of himself is harsh, as is his representation of reading. In place of the lively give-and-take in the conversations with Jack McFarland that made books and ideas come alive for Rose, Rogriguez has a series of tick marks made on a list of books read alone.

Whereas he admired the nuns who taught him in elementary school and whose "personas" he wished to "assume," he feels no such admiration for the academics he encounters as a graduate student. His description of the life of the academic is less than complimentary as he describes the "dour faces" of his "community of scholars" (69). He further describes his fellow occupants of the reading room of the British Museum, the regulars who "chatter madly" to themselves, as having faces "worn by long study" (70). He writes, "I seemed unable to dare a passionate statement. I felt drawn by professionalism to the edge of sterility, capable of no more than pedantic, lifeless, unassailable prose" (73). Here, Rodriguez is pretty much at the end of his "long, unglamorous, even demeaning process" of education (68). His experience with graduate study is not dissimilar to Rose's: both quit graduate school when they could no longer see any point to continuing; the "life," the excitement of being involved in a conversation bigger than oneself now appears reduced to a monologue, an audience of one writer and a dissertation committee. Rose reenergizes himself by quitting and joining Teacher Corps to teach students with backgrounds similar to his own. He seems not to see his experience of intellectual paralysis as inherent to academia itself in general but, rather, to himself in particular. Rodriguez, however, argues that such sterility is the fate of the scholarship boy, and he leaves academia and teaching entirely and begins to "long for his past" (69). And, unlike Rose whose career can be seen as directly connecting to his own experiences of school and schooling, Rodriguez states that "there is no specific pedagogy to glean" from his story (68). Rose remains passionately committed to the teacher's responsibility to "invite" students into the "conversation," to open the doors to the academy as wide as possible. Rodriguez, on the other hand, remains ambivalent, and some of his critics charge that he attempts to close the academy's doors to students of color because of his opposition to affirmative action and bilingual education.

By the end of *Hunger of Memory*, the academy holds no allure. What had seemed desirable to the child appears suffocating to the man. Rowe writes:

> To the student from a working-class background, the middle-class academic world seems to offer significant freedoms and opportunities for expression, which may be limited by what that student may see as prejudices, superstitions, and other narrownesses associated with the home culture. However, this time, as in the case of Rodriguez, there is often a process of disillusionment with this new world. It has its own narrownesses, its own blinders, its own limiting preconceptions and repressions even though they may be expressed more subtly or in different ways from those at home. (230)

As Rodriguez turns his back on academia, he turns his gaze more sharply on what he has lost. But by the time he becomes acutely aware of that loss, it appears to be too late. At the end of his narrative, Rodriguez realizes his father has spoken to him only once at the very end of their family's Christmas gathering and that is to ask if he is "going home now too." There is no real connection between them other than genetic, and Rodriguez offers no indication that this will change. Yet after his formal education ends, his real education begins as he is able to resee his parents with great perception and sensitivity. As part of his own story, he tells his parents' stories as well and now is able to admire and appreciate who they are and what they gave up for their children. Rowe writes:

> His parents are presented in such a way as to demonstrate their considerable capacities, but also to show how institutions have failed them. . . . Rodriguez is aware, as are often other working-class offspring, of the seriousness of his parents, people who have shouldered major responsibility from an early age, and whose childhood and youth were brief or non-existent by middle-class standards. The authority of experience leads the working-class academic to the conclusion that he or she doesn't have greater mental or moral merit than relatives or friends on the other side, even though educational institutions encourage that meritocratic view. (206–7)

Rodriguez describes his parents with little sentimentalism but much admiration, yet his representation of his family and of his relationship with them is what so many of the students in my classes have objected to. Many come from working-class backgrounds so they cannot know the distance to which higher education will carry them away from family and friends. They resist the possibility that education can change them to such an extent, and so they resist Rodriguez.

Of course, others find Rodriguez's narrative problematic as well. Victor Villanueva in his own memoir and literacy narrative *Bootstraps: From an American Academic of Color*, for example, writes, "Like many a Latino, I was upset by Richard Rodriguez's autobiography, *Hunger of Memory*, but I did understand . . ." (39). Villanueva makes clear that Rodriguez's story itself does not trouble him; rather, "[i]t was the melancholy, the ideological resignation, the way he seemed not to see that biculturalism is as imposed as assimilation" (39). He defines *biculturalism* as "the tensions within, which are caused by being unable to deny the old or the new. Rodriguez struggles at denying the tension, and when he cannot (his hungering memory), he says that is just how it is; it's okay in the long run" (39). In other words, Villanueva is arguing that Rodriguez is saying that the loss of this connection to his family and past is the natural result of assimilation, that "this great expense is simply the cost of becoming an American" (xvi). However, Villanueva points out the irony that "for all [Rodriguez's] fame as an American writing in English about assimilation, his attempts at assimilation failed. He is called upon to explain the Latino; he has not melted into the American pot" (xvi).

While Villanueva cannot agree with Rodriguez that this tension is the price to be paid ("that is just how it is") and resents that tension in his own life, my students, on the other hand, tend to cling to the belief that they will feel no tension whatsoever. However, those from working-class backgrounds with strong, affectionate ties to home and family most likely need to be prepared for that tension as Min Zhan Lu argues in "Redefining the Legacy of Mina Shaughnessy." Lu's article argues that Shaughnessy's understanding of learning and appropriating Standard English is flawed. Shaughnessy is aware that students might resist acquiring discursive practices that would mark them as alien to their home environments, yet she resists or cannot entertain the possibility that those same discursive practices might serve to alienate her students and their families and friends from each other. Shaughnessy recommends that teachers make use of a "formal" over a "contextual" approach to teaching language and usage. The example Lu offers from Shaughnessy's *Errors and Expectations* is the teaching of suffixes and prefixes as a kind of stealth approach to teaching students to acquire an "academic vocabulary." Lu argues that Shaughnessy is naïve; language shapes us; changing how we speak and write changes who we are. But students will most likely not realize they have changed until after the fact, and "because the classroom has suggested that learning academic discourse will not affect how they think, feel, or relate to home, students are also likely to perceive their 'betrayal' of home as purely personal choices" (113). In other words, they may blame themselves for any sense of separation they feel. Lu draws from Rodriguez's narrative to make her argument:

> Rodriguez's narrative also suggests that the best way for students to cope constructively with their sense of having consented to a 'betrayal' is to perceive it in relation to the politics of education and language. . . . When students are encouraged to pay attention to the ways in which diverse discourses constrain one's alignments with different points of view and social groups, they have a better chance to deliberate over how they might resist various pressures academic discourse exercises on their existing points of view. (113)

So although students may resist the conclusions Rodriguez draws from his experience, reading, discussing, and writing in response to his conclusions may also serve to help them in these "deliberations."

Someone like I, eager to shake off any and all working-class markers, embraced discursive changes and, I am not pleased to admit, experienced the widening rifts between me and my parents as signs of my parents' failures. Although I am not proud of my eagerness to distance myself from my "roots," I understand some of my motivations and feel none of Rodriguez's nostalgia. I was not "an enchantedly happy child" (Rodriguez 3). But students with stronger identifications with home and family benefit from some preparation for the changes they face, as Lu suggests. Yet Dana C. Elder reminds us in his opinion piece in *College English* that our background is not our students' backgrounds—even when those backgrounds can be labeled working class. Rather than trying to prove our "bona fides" by telling our own stories of struggle and change, he advises that we instead "model optimism, to value and praise, and to limit autobiographical revelations to the present" (569–70). He continues, "Somehow we teachers, with the help of our peers and our students, need to design and build a new and broader staircase that all can use. The building materials must be abstract as well as autobiographical, must take their substance from both the personal and the universally human" (570). I would add the importance of reminding teachers—working class, middle class, elite, whatever—of the many ways difference manifests itself. We have much to learn from immersing ourselves in literacy narratives.

Chapter Three

Identity, Class, and Higher Literacy
Theories of Literacy, Ways of Knowing

A FEW YEARS AGO AT THE Conference on College Composition and Communication, one of the panelists on working-class issues, Caroline Pari, revealed
in the question-and-answer session after her presentation that, whereas she
was an avid reader completing her Ph.D. in English, her identical twin sister
was just as avid a nonreader. In fact, Pari is the only member of her working-class family to pursue higher education or higher literacy. Conventional
wisdom says that a book-rich environment will produce children more likely
to be highly literate and that a book-poor environment will produce children
more likely to experience difficulty in school—and perhaps beyond. So Pari is
a seeming anomaly. I was struck by Pari's story because it resembles something
of my own background as a passionate reader in a working-class household of
indifferent, infrequent readers. In a certain sense, my project in writing this
book is an effort to make sense of that anomaly if, indeed, it is an anomaly. In
other words, I want to ask why some, especially those from seemingly unlikely
backgrounds, determinedly seek higher literacy against all expectations and
predictions, whereas others do not. This chapter synthesizes current literacy,
composition, and class theories to begin to answer this question.

An impulse operates in composition pedagogy to see literacy in emancipatory terms. The grand narrative of literacy is that it will enable prosperity
and critical awareness. The work of Northrop Frye and Louise Rosenblatt has
argued that reading literature makes it possible for students to see and appreciate other cultures and their own humanistic connections to people from those

She's
looking
at variations.

45

cultures. In the Arnoldian tradition, Allan Bloom has argued in *The Closing of the American Mind* that reading great works of literature with sensitivity and with the right attitude (respectful, not deconstructive) will create a worthy citizenry; the wrong kind of literacy, however, threatens to "close" our minds. E. D. Hirsch's *Cultural Literacy* had enormous impact in the 1980s offering a list of "what literate Americans know" and arguing that we are in danger of cultural chaos because we cannot communicate in the ways his own father and his contemporaries did.

On the left, literacy fills the same emancipatory function in different terms. Antonio Gramsci called for the working class to receive the same education as elites to work toward their own liberation. Paulo Freire, imprisoned and exiled for his work with Brazilian peasants, argued in *Pedagogy of the Oppressed* for literacy training that would enable peasants to develop consciousness of their oppression and then work to overcome it. Ira Shor and Henry Giroux, influenced by Freire, worked throughout their careers to create student-centered classrooms in which students can take responsibility for their own literacy training and, ultimately, their own critical and political awareness. Geneva Smitherman and others have called for schools to make the effort to understand and work from an understanding of black vernacular English to help black students see the connections and differences between it and Standard English. And bell hooks "teaches to transgress."

Given how we as teachers, no matter our pedagogical politics, are committed to enabling our students' efforts to become more highly literate, paying attention to teachers' stories of their own literacy acquisition is helpful to understand something of their assumptions about the worth of literacy. I am particularly drawn to working-class literacy narratives because I teach at a university where many students, undergraduate and graduate alike, are first-generation college students and because of my own working-class background. How do teachers from nonelite backgrounds describe their own desires for and efforts to achieve higher literacy? What can we learn from these descriptions?

Shirley Brice Heath's *Ways with Words: Language, Life, and Work in Communities and Classrooms* helps us see the ways that class and race contribute to our successes or failures in school and with school literacy. Interestingly, however, she predicts readers will want to see race as a key factor in literacy acquisition even though class figures as a far bigger factor. In other words, class plays a bigger role in literacy acquisition than race. Heath:

> argues that in Roadville and Trackton the different ways children learned to use language were dependent on the ways in which each community structured their families, defined the roles that community members could assume, and played out their concepts of childhood that guided child socialization. . . . The place of language in the cultural life of each social group is

interdependent with the habits and values of behaving shared among members of that group (11).

Over a ten-year period, Heath worked closely among the communities that are the object of her ethnographic study, describing in specific detail how language is used and taught, making clear that no language deficit exists in the two working-class communities. Language is shared, valued, and transmitted there, but it is shared, valued, and transmitted differently. However, the townspeople's ways of transmitting language are most valued in the school system and, therefore, lead to their greater success in acquiring school literacy. Heath warns, "unless the boundaries between classrooms and communities can be broken, and the flow of cultural patterns between them encouraged, the schools will continue to legitimate and reproduce communities of townspeople who control and limit the potential progress of other communities and who themselves remain untouched by other values and ways of life" (369). Of course, little is being done to encourage that "flow of cultural patterns" and students from backgrounds similar to Roadville and Trackton still find themselves at a linguistic disadvantage.

Deborah Brandt's work has done much to learn more about this "flow" and about literacy acquisition across generations, classes, and racial and ethnic groups. In interviews, she learned how literate practices are very much a part of virtually everyone's home and working lives and to what lengths individuals will go to become increasingly literate, even those individuals whom we do not necessarily see as more than marginally literate. In her article "Sponsors of Literacy" and in her book *Literacy in American Lives*, Brandt demonstrates how her interviewees, especially those from working-class backgrounds, work to stay ahead of the literacy demands of their jobs. For example, Dwayne Lowery finds that to be effective as a union representative, he continuously has to learn increasingly complex literacy practices to keep up with the changes management uses to keep the upper hand in contract negotiations.

Brandt observes that a key component to a person's literacy acquisition is a sponsor, which she defines "as any agents, local or distant, concrete or abstract, who enable, support, teach, model, as well as recruit, regulate, suppress or withhold literacy—and gain advantage in it in some way." She goes on to explain:

> [a]lthough the interests of the sponsor and the sponsored do not have to converge (and, in fact, may conflict) sponsors nevertheless set the terms for access to literacy and wield powerful incentives for compliance and loyalty. Sponsors are a tangible reminder that literacy learning throughout history has always required permission, sanction, assistance, coercion, or at minimum, contact with existing trade routes." ("Sponsors" 166–7)

Brandt uncovers, building on Heath's work, that literacy is not equally available in the same ways to all. Juxtaposing Dolores Lopez, a working-class

Latina of immigrant parents, and Raymond Branch, a white, middle-class child of professional parents, she shows how their access or lack of access to the manifestations of literacy (in this example, largely represented as computer knowledge and comfort) clearly affects the trajectory of their lives. Branch is the son of a computer science professor and, from his earliest memories, he had access to computers, to computer labs, to people highly knowledgeable about computers, and to the expectation that he, too, would be highly knowledgeable about computers. In other words, compared to Lopez, he had a head start. Lopez, on the other hand, had to play a continual game of catch-up. She is bilingual because her parents' first language is Spanish; when she and her family become aware of the importance of computer skills to economic (and linguistic) success in this country, her parents find the means to buy her a used word processor. By the time Brandt interviewed Lopez, she has a job of which she is proud and that she performs proudly, but she is still, and will most likely always be, behind Branch, who has a lucrative job in terms of job income and status in the computer field.

Brandt and Heath both account for the inhibitions and obstacles to higher literacy among those with working-class backgrounds. Yet what of those who have managed to overcome those inhibitions? What stories are told about their desire for and acquisition of higher literacy? In *Landscape for a Good Woman*, Carolyn Steedman uses the stories of her and her mother's childhoods and lives to describe "lives for which the central interpretive devices of the culture don't quite work" (5). The grand narratives, as well as research Heath, Brandt, and others have conducted, tell us that working-class children, as a rule, do not desire higher literacy. Some, such as Patrick J. Finn in *Literacy with an Attitude: Educating Working-Class Children in Their Own Self-Interest*, argue:

> [o]ver time, political, social, and economic forces have brought us to a place where the working class (and to a surprising degree, the middle class) gets domesticating education and functional literacy, and the rich get empowering education and powerful literacy. We don't worry about a literate working class because the kind of literacy they get doesn't make them dangerous. (x)

In other words, according to Finn, working-class children are covertly educated to be working class. Rick Bragg's memoir *All Over But the Shoutin'* offers the example of Bragg's older brother Sam:

> The principal and teachers, when they recognized who we were, where we ranked, told Sam that he could sweep the narrow halls, clean the bathrooms and shovel coal into the school's furnace, to earn his free lunch. He took out the trash and burned it and unclogged the toilet. They never bothered to teach him to read very well; he learned that on his own. They never bothered to tell him about the world outside his narrow, limited one. They forgot to show him maps of the universe or share the secrets of history, biology. As

other students behind the classroom doors read about about [*sic*] empires, wars and kings, he waxed the gymnasium floor. (104)

Sam had been "recognized" by his teachers as working class, and, as a result, they felt little responsibility to offer him what little was available by way of education.

Of course, we know that many "escape" the grand narrative and go on to tell their own story of that "escape" in whatever form it takes. Literacy narratives necessarily tell stories of success—otherwise why write or read them—and when the writer is from a working-class background that success generally figures as "escape" from the fate that the larger narrative would seem to indicate was to be their destiny. Steedman writes, "Personal interpretations of past time—the stories that people tell themselves in order to explain how they got to the place they currently inhabit—are often in deep and ambiguous conflict with the official interpretive devices of a culture" (6). What interests me is how "the stories that people tell themselves in order to explain how they got to the place they currently inhabit" describe their desire for and acquisition of higher literacy and what teachers might use or, more important, learn not to use in their own work with their own students.

Certainly our backgrounds, the social and economic conditions in which we lived and grew, shape our readings, and in the interest of revealing something of what shapes my reading of this research and the literacy narratives that follow, I want to describe briefly something of my own literacy narrative. My parents had jobs, not careers. My father grew up on a farm, dropped out of high school, and, although he spent time when I was in junior high and high school wearing a white shirt and tie (that is, he was promoted to retail credit manager), he began as a milkman and retired as a dock foreman, all for the same large milk company. My mother finished high school and, for a time before my birth, enjoyed reading popular novels (an Edna Ferber novel from this period sat for decades on a small book shelf among *Reader's Digest* condensed novels until her recent move to a retirement community). For most of my early childhood, she was able to stay at home, yet as more and more Latinos moved into our working-class neighborhood, my parents became increasingly eager to move to a "nicer" neighborhood. She began working for a company that does telephone consumer surveys and stayed with that same company until she retired shortly after my father's death.

Literacy was largely centered on the newspaper, to which my parents always subscribed, *Guideposts* (which I have no memory of anyone actually reading), and *Reader's Digest.* My father also picked up magazines such as *Inside Detective,* which were kept in his nightstand and were off limits to me although I easily found ways to read them. I have no memories of being read to; however, my mother insists that she read to me with great regularity from the time I was brought home from the hospital. I did not learn to read early, but once I started first grade (kindergarten was not available), I caught on quickly, and I just as quickly became a voracious reader. Again, my mother encouraged me by taking me regularly to the public library. As an overweight, unathletic, not particularly attractive child, I soon used reading as an escape from the real world, a world that, for large periods of time, was markedly unhappy as I grew older and my father's alcoholism worsened. During those difficult times, literacy was not just pleasure; it was survival. And later it became a means for dissociating from my parents as I went on to college and various jobs and, ultimately, an academic career. This is not to say my family life was utterly miserable or that I was abused, but it was not an "enchantedly happy childhood" and reading provided much of the pleasure that I remember.

Therefore, as I read, I am drawn to literacy narratives such as mine that feature a perceived escape from a flawed childhood, and I find no scarcity of such narratives. For example, Roxanne Dunbar-Ortiz (no relation), in her wonderful memoir *Red Dirt: Growing Up Okie*, describes her hardscrabble childhood with a loving but periodically violent family, including a mother whose escalating mental illness forced its disintegration. Yet that same mother taught her that she could be anything she set her mind to be, including president, and taught her to value "storying": "'You just make up whatever you want to be,'" her mother told her (41). Her older brother Laurence also taught her to value literacy; after he teaches her the derivation of the word *buck* (meaning one dollar), he tells her, "'I found it in a book. Everything has an explanation, Roxie. You have to ask the question and then find the answer in a book'" (55).

Both school and reading serve as escapes from her increasingly troubled and violent family and from her limitations because of asthma. Teachers, on the whole, prove to be sources of both solace and knowledge as one teacher, without prying into her home life, takes her home to her own book-lined house and opens her up to such "radical" (and banned in Oklahoma at the time) books as *The Grapes of Wrath*. Dunbar-Ortiz makes straight *A*'s and counts the days until she can finish high school and leave her home. Several years later, now married, Dunbar-Ortiz describes her reading as no longer being for escape but for "knowledge" as she tries to make sense of her own life, of her in-laws' attitudes toward her, and class divisions that affect her immediate world. She even claims that reading cured her problems with migraines and insomnia: "It was then that I realized that self-knowledge and education are curatives, and it was then I believe that I determined to become a teacher one day" (207). And it is literacy, a surreptitious reading of a letter from one in-law to another describing her as "white trash" likely to drag the whole family "down to her level" (213), that opens her eyes to the class division in her own married life, launches her out of Oklahoma and, ultimately, to a doctorate from UCLA and an academic career.

Rick Bragg's *All Over But the Shoutin'* also tells the story of a rural, working-class childhood that would be unlikely to produce the Pulitzer Prize–winning writer he became. Bragg's narrative honors his mother and the sacrifices she made to raise him and his two brothers, doing what she could to protect them from poverty and from their abusive father. He clearly communicates how much his mother loved him and how much he respects and loves her in return, but this narrative, too, is an escape narrative. Different from his two brothers—one will live a life of honest manual labor, one will end up in prison—Bragg describes himself as a:

> dreamer, and while I loved the woods and the creeks and the natural bounty of our world, I also loved to bury myself in books. After all the lights were shut out, I would cover up my head, click on the flashlight, and read as long as the batteries lasted from *You Were There* books about the Alamo, the Creek Indian Wars, the Battle of New Orleans. I solved mysteries with the Hardy Boys, and drifted down the Mississippi with Mark Twain. By the time I was in the eighth grade, I had read every book—except the ones for the little kids—in the tiny library at Roy Webb Junior High School. I am not bragging. I was just hungry. (91)

From an early age, he is aware of the class differences between his family and those from "the other side" whose "cars . . . don't tinkle with the sound of rolling beer bottles, and houses that don't have a bed in the living room" (98). He writes:

> All I had to do was look across the Formica-topped kitchen table to my brother Sam, to see my future. At thirteen, he had done a man's job shoveling coal, pushing a wheelbarrow loaded with rocks, mucking out hog pens, loading boxcars at Dixie Clay with an endless line of fifty-pound bags of clay and lime. Some nights he would go to sleep sitting in that hard-backed chair, and Momma would lead him to bed. The work was his birthright. (99)

Bragg knows this is not what he wants to see as his own birthright, but with few models to guide him to alternatives, he very nearly wastes what little opportunity he has with a *C* average and no real focus for his desires other than knowing what he does not want. His knack for writing and his "charmed life" lead him to high school journalism, and after he is briefly but terrifyingly questioned as a murder suspect, he enrolls in one journalism class at Jacksonville State University: "It would be the first step, the first act, in a series of moves and machinations—most of them involving dumb, blind luck—that would give me what I was searching for" (121) That first step leads to a job with the *New York Times* and the Pulitzer Prize, and in the conclusion to his narrative, higher literacy in the form of the Pulitzer Prize becomes the ultimate validation to "shove . . . down the throats of the people who questioned my sophistication, my very existence among them" (306). (Unfortunately, Bragg later lost the award because he was said to have plagiarized.)

"Literacy salvaged my life. It is as simple and fundamental as that" (xiii) begins the preface of Sharon Jean Hamilton's literacy narrative *My Name's Not Susie: A Life Transformed by Literacy*. Daughter of a prostitute, Hamilton spent the first three years of her life in her abusive home, multiple foster homes, and an orphanage. At the age of three-and-a-half, she was adopted by a family who had problems of their own but who encouraged her to read and write. Hamilton is very clear to name literacy as the means of her escape from a horrific childhood and of her ultimate survival:

> Reading and writing provided both a way out of my own misery and a way into understanding the sources of that misery. At first, literacy provided escape from the real world, where there seemed to be no place for me, into a fantasy world of love and adventure. However, as I kept reading and writing, I learned a very different kind of escape. Literacy equipped me with the knowledge and confidence to decide how I would live my life as the kind of person I wanted to be. We hear a lot about the importance of literacy, primarily in functional terms of day-to-day living and preparation for the world of work. Those roles are undeniable. But literacy also plays a powerful role in the interior working-out of who we are and how we decide what will be the conduct of our day-to-day lives. (xiv)

I quote at length here because Hamilton spells out clearly a common assumption about the power of reading and writing many hold who see literacy as the key not only to their economic and educational success, but also to their very existence. Reading and writing enable her to transcend abuse as a child and class as an adult. The move that follows is Hamilton's assumption that the same is true for all, that is, that literacy can serve that function for everyone.

Interestingly, Hamilton herself, in retrospect, sees the ways that her quest for higher literacy comes as a result of her not fitting in among others in her classes in school and her efforts ensured that she would never fit in. At one point, she literally does not fit in as the principal has to take her from class to class, trying to find a spare desk and reinforcing her sense of being a "displaced person." Desperate for approval on some level or another, she vows that she will become the top student in each subject:

> In making this vow, I was completely unaware that I was selling out my love of learning for an ephemeral label and setting myself up for failure, not to mention the increased contempt of my classmates. Even as I gradually became aware of the cost over the ensuing months and years, I counted it value for the price. Top marks became my goal and my solace; they were the only way I knew how to be special. (56)

Higher literacy becomes a goal in and of itself, largely as a result of her not knowing any other means of seeking or finding approval. Throughout a life of struggle and scholarship, Hamilton ultimately earns a doctorate and a teaching job, where she reproduces her own attitudes toward literacy with her students. She writes:

> As I read my students' forays into their wildernesses, they read mine. It is an open invitation for my students to see that literacy, that writing—others' as well as their own—is a way to understand not just their positions and perspectives in their world but also how and why they arrived at those positions and perspectives, and why and how they might wish to maintain them or to change them. It may provide, for some, a small flame of inspiration to see that the gap between the lives they lead and the lives they want to lead is surmountable. The gap can be crossed, and literacy is one means of enabling this to happen. (147)

She recounts stories of her students' (interestingly, all the examples are women) writing about their own abuse, divorce, and other hardship, and the book ends with another literacy-as-escape narrative by one of those students. She is valuing the stories that most closely resemble her own, and I find this disturbing. What are the implications for our pedagogy if we reproduce what Heath, Brandt, Dunbar-Ortiz, Bragg, and Hamilton, as well as others, have called into question: that is, that middle-class teachers reward the middle-class students most like themselves? Yet here is Hamilton doing the same with her students. In addition, I have to ask what happens to the students who fit neither model, students such as the majority with whom I work each semester, students who come from relatively happy homes and had relatively good experiences in school. They are more likely to perceive literacy as a chore or job than as escape or survival. They are the ones who struggle to think of what to write about and who generally have more difficulty connecting themselves to their texts. And how can the relatively happy, well-adjusted student match in drama what the troubled student (who is willing to reveal those troubles) can produce?

Not surprisingly, the students in my study asked to tell stories about their own literacy acquisition had far more mixed responses than the published previously cited narratives. Most hold warm memories of being read to and of their first efforts to learn to read, but when the subject was writing, the responses were far more mixed. Michael (who asked that his last name not be used), for example, recalls "the highlight of my kindergarten year was being placed in the top reading group, the Blue Jays." His story details his mother's loving efforts to teach him to read and write at age three so that by the time he began school, he was well ahead of the others and exulted in being "the best reader in the Blue Jays. Yes, I was the best in the class." He concludes by observing that "[n]ow my reading and writing are average, but along the way,

I have discovered new talents that I never would have known existed without that first competitive spark so many years ago. Through my own efforts, triumphs and failures, and [sic] identity has been formed, and I like what I see." Michael, although no longer considering himself a "top" reader and writer, still sees his literacy acquisition in positive terms and sees literacy as opening pathways for other talents and interests.

Other students write in positive terms about the writing they do to express themselves, to clarify their thinking to themselves, to sort out their feelings and are careful to mark this kind of writing as different and more pleasurable than academic writing. For instance, Catherine Canzoneri writes:

> Writing is mostly a way for me to express my feelings. While I do write for academic reasons, I've found that I seem to enjoy writing better when I have no guidelines and I'm not being graded on what I write. Most of the time, I write when I need to get things off my chest. I don't always write it in the same way. Sometimes I write poems, other times I write letters, other times I feel like writing letters, even if they are not intended to be read by someone else. This tends to help me explain things when I feel like I am talking directly to someone. Writing is a way for me to shape my own reality and to mold it into what I want it to be.

Kimberly Dunham describes her attitudes toward writing similarly:

> When I write I feel . . . like I can express myself. I can write and describe how I am feeling, or a situation, or anything that I feel the need to write about. I like to write, especially when there are no limitations on what I can write about. I prefer writing when there isn't a topic or even when there is a topic but it's a broad topic and I can use my imagination. I don't like to write when I have a specific topic or a specific subject that I have to write about. I don't like being limited on what I am writing about. When I write I feel . . . like I can make my feelings or emotions understandable.

White, middle-class students, Michael, Catherine, and Kimberly feel largely positive about their literacy experiences—especially when they are in control of why and what they write.

The majority of students in my sample, however, describe their efforts to achieve higher literacy in less positive terms. Marcus Lane writes, for example, "When I write I feel that I am just occupying time. At this point I have no feeling towards writing but I hope through this class and over time [I] can learn to like writing." Julie Watson writes of her frustration:

> When I write, I feel confused because I know I can write about anything but choosing something to write about is really hard. I sometimes know what to write about but I just don't know how to say it. The words seem to slip away sometimes. I am very indecisive and never know what to do. I always

try to write about events or certain topics which others can enjoy and relate to. I like to write but don't always like others to read it because I sometimes think it may not be good enough. Every time I write, I feel that it's not good enough and that it never will be. I try to overcome this feeling but it just doesn't work.

Watson, to my way of thinking, does an eloquent job describing how many of us feel about our efforts to get our words down on paper or screen, but that doesn't diminish the frustration she obviously experiences. Representing the most negative experience with writing, Nick Monday writes:

> When I write, I feel like someone is pointing a gun to my head. The only reason I ever write is because I have to, usually for school purposes. I never was a good writer and usually when they make us write the grade has more weight and hurts my average more and more. The only time I feel good when writing is when I am finished and can just forget about it.

What most of these students are saying is that the only time they might possibly experience writing as pleasurable is when they are writing to tell a story they want to tell or writing privately to explore their own feelings. As Brandt demonstrates through her many case studies with children and young adults:

> . . . young authors of stories and poems used technical knowledge derived from their reading to make their compositions, but it is noteworthy that the motivations for the writing in these cases were not books and the motivators were not adults. Rather, the occasions and impulses to write emerged from the children's immediate circumstances and feelings. Whereas people tended to remember reading for the sensual and emotional pleasure that it gave, they tended to remember writing for the pain or isolation it was meant to assuage." (*Literacy* 154–5)

Very simply put, reading is remembered with pleasure; writing is far more likely to be associated with "troubles" (*Literacy* 167).

Almost twenty years after *Ways with Words*, in his *College Composition and Communication* article "School Sucks," T. R. Johnson charges that we as educators are complicit in our students' being turned off to school in general and writing in particular. He writes, "By embarrassing students [by our relentless marking of their errors], we slowly but surely initiate them into a certain set of affiliations, into a kind of membership that, as Patricia Bizzell and Richard Rodriguez both note, can unfold as a painful repudiation of their home culture" and that become, over years of literacy education, linked, "perhaps indelibly, to pain" (632). So school literacy starts off in favor of middle-class children, and as Johnson argues, the ways literacy is taught continue to "sour" whatever pleasure most students may have taken from their literacy education. Johnson's concern is that our teaching methods may have played a role in increasing school violence. In my foregoing critique of Hamilton, I am in no way suggesting that we should discourage students from expressing their concerns, pains, and traumas, but reading the stories of successful literacy acquisition alongside students' descriptions of their attitudes toward their own efforts to become more highly literate prompts me to ask: What can we as teachers do to resist what I call the pedagogy of the "mini-me"? How do we turn the camera on ourselves to see who and what we reward and punish in our classrooms?

Contemporary literacy theory teaches us that literacy is not innocent. Heath's ethnographic research reveals how literacy training in whatever forms and patterns begins literally during a baby's first days. Brandt's work shows us that access to higher literacy is always assisted or "sponsored" in some form or another. In *Social Linguistics and Literacies: Ideology in Discourses*, James Paul Gee shows us the ways that access to higher literacy must be conceived in terms of its plural nature, that is, "Literacy is always multiple: there are literacies, each of which involves control of Discourses involving print" (xviii), and that it is achieved through a kind of apprenticeship that implies that in addition to learning ways of using language, the apprentice also learns ways of being, acting, and valuing. In other words, literacy and ideology are inextricably tied. He writes:

> In the end, we might say that, contrary to the literacy myth, *nothing* follows from schooling. Much follows, however, from what comes *with* literacy and schooling, what literacy and schooling come wrapped up in, namely the attitudes, values, norms and beliefs (at once social, cultural and political) that always accompany literacy and schooling. These consequences may be work habits that facilitate industrialization, abilities in "expository talk in contrived situations," a religiously or politically quiescent population, radical opposition to colonial oppressors, and any number of other things. A text, whether written on paper, or on the soul (Plato), or on the world (Freire), is a loaded weapon. The person, the educator, who hands over the gun, hands over the bullets (the perspective), and must own up to the consequences. There is no way out of having an opinion, an ideology, and a strong one, as did Plato, as does Freire. Literacy education is not for the timid. (42)

So Nick Monday's feeling of someone holding a gun to his head is far more perceptive than we might have first thought.

According to Gee, literacy comes in a package, and the higher the literacy, the more that is included in that package. Monday is well aware that more is being asked of him than just to learn to read and write "better." Gee goes on to explain:

> The teacher of English is not, in fact, teaching English, and certainly not English grammar, or even "language." Rather, she is teaching a set of discourse

practices, oral and written connected with the standard dialect of English. More importantly, she is apprenticing students to dominant, school-based practices. Language and literacy acquisition are forms of socialization, in this case socialization into mainstream ways of using language in speech and print, mainstream ways of taking meaning, and of making sense of experience. (67)

On some level, students are aware that if they take on the ways of using language the teacher is requiring, they will be changed. The struggle is great enough if the apprentice is willing (I am thinking of my own struggles in graduate school here); it is greater still when the apprentice is suspicious or unwilling, as in Monday's case. Yet what is even more problematic is when the teacher herself is unaware of what she is asking of her students or when she can see the apprenticeship only in light of what she sees in positive terms of her own choice to be socialized as in the previous case of Hamilton.

What is called for is a radical self-awareness, a self-awareness that calls into question the assumptions those of us from nonmainstream backgrounds may have internalized in the process of our own apprenticeships. In the process of entering the middle class, we need to ask ourselves what values and norms have become invisible. Nancy Grimm calls this process "relentless reflection." In *Good Intentions: Writing Center Work for Postmodern Times*, she writes:

> The literacy myth teaches us to think of literacy as an unequivocally good thing, something that improves a person's position in life. The achievement of advanced literacy is supposed to make us better people, better citizens, and better workers, especially in the information age when so much work depends on the ability to manage information. When literacy is conceptualized only in positive, mythical terms, we lose sight of its paradoxical effects. When I was a child, my mother often urged me "[to] get your nose out of books for a while" because she wanted her daughter to participate in the real life around her, not just the manufactured life on the pages of books. On an intuitive level my mother understood the paradox of literacy: it both connects and separates, liberates and controls, empowers and limits. While books may extend a child's horizons, they simultaneously limit her interactions with daily life. (39)

As Richard Rodriguez's much-cited autobiography *Hunger of Memory* teaches us, literacy gains can also be personal losses as the student becomes socialized in ways foreign to his or her familial values and norms.

Brandt refers to teachers as "conflicted brokers of literacy," meaning that, whether we like it, we operate within the rhetoric of economic equality, knowing that such equality is far more myth than reality for our students from working-class backgrounds. Heath's work in Roadville and Trackton make visible the ways that teachers' class backgrounds blind them to many of their own prejudices and how those prejudices affect perceptions of what knowledge is valued and what knowledge is labeled deficient or deviant. Her ethnographic research and her work in the community's schools helped the teachers she worked with reflect on those prejudices and see many of the ways they filtered into their interpretations and evaluations of students' classroom performances. Experts largely assumed that the white middle-class teacher is most in need of such reflection. I contend, however, that teachers from working-class backgrounds must reflect on how their teaching, too, is colored by their literacy acquisition and that their own motivations and experiences can produce prejudices leading them to disabling assumptions about their students as well. Although I am not calling for full ethnographic studies of our students' literacy backgrounds, I am arguing that we need to take time to learn something about our students' attitudes toward reading and writing, both the reading and writing they did as children and the reading and writing they anticipate doing for us in our classrooms, and to juxtapose those literacy stories with our own literacy narratives.

Chapter Four

Metaphors We Write By

IN the first act of David Mamet's play *Oleanna*, John, the pompous professor, says to Carol, the difficult student, "That's my job—to provoke you." Carol responds, puzzled, "To make me mad is your job?" Many of us trained to value critical inquiry and to push our students to question assumptions and ask difficult questions would most likely concur with John, and "pushing" students to work harder in their writing and thinking is a metaphor I frequently use in teaching and teacher training. We assume that students will perceive this metaphor in positive terms, that they will automatically understand that we have only good intentions to make them better critical thinkers, writers, and readers.

Yet Carol's perplexed response is worth taking the time to consider. She doesn't share John's metaphorical understanding of "provoke." Provocation is not, after all, a neutral term; self defense is in many cases an appropriate response to provocation. In John and Carol's case, their readings and misreadings of each other's words—that is, each other's metaphors—lead to disastrous results. So why is John surprised when Carol resists and resents being provoked? Why are we surprised when students do not share our metaphors?

In *Metaphors We Live By*, George Lakoff and Mark Johnson argue that metaphors reflect our "conceptual system," the system that "plays a central role in defining our everyday realities." They continue, "If we are right in suggesting that our conceptual system is largely metaphorical, then the way we think, what we experience, and what we do every day is very much a matter of metaphor" (3). Or as John Berger concisely states in *Ways of Seeing*, "What we know shapes what we see" (4). We as teachers need to take time to learn something of our students' attitudes toward the acquisition of higher literacy via their representations of that acquisition in literacy narratives and their metaphors for their perceptions of that acquisition. Then we can juxtapose those literacy stories with our own to reflect on the pedagogical assumptions we bring into the classroom. Specifically, I want to bring together literacy narratives and metaphors first-year writing students and first-year teaching and graduate assistants write to expand what teachers know about their students' as well as their own reading and writing. I am arguing that such juxtaposition enables us to see in more complex ways what impedes or motivates the acquisition of higher literacy.

As stated earlier, published literacy narratives can teach us much about the motives and desires of successful writers. Student-produced literacy narratives can teach us much about what turns off some students to reading and writing as they work their ways through years of schooling and about what works for the students who make it to college and beyond, ready to tackle more demanding literacy practices. As Mary Soliday explains in "Translating Self and Difference through Literacy Narratives":

> At the most basic level, the plot of a literacy story tells what happens when we acquire language, either spoken or written. But literacy stories are also places where writers explore what Victor Turner calls "liminal" crossings between worlds. In focusing on those moments when the self is on the threshold of possible intellectual, social, and emotional development, literacy narratives become sites of self-translation where writers can articulate the meanings and the consequences of their passages between language worlds. (511)

In other words, literacy narratives can help students become interpreters of their own experience once that experience is "de-naturalized" and becomes a subject of study in itself. Soliday argues that such study will reveal to both student and teacher the potential for empowerment as they see the successful negotiations students make between languages and discourses:

> If students and teachers begin to see their languages as mutually shaping, they also recognize their double-voicedness and, in so doing, can see the self as rooted in other cultures yet also belonging to, becoming transformed by, and in turn transforming school cultures. Instead of being seen as outsiders who must choose to write either from within or against the academy, students assume a position of strength. (522)

Soliday offers an optimistic picture in which teachers see students' ways of using language as informing and enriching academic discourses and in which students see their ways of using language and themselves as capable of such transformations.

Certainly, students need to "assume a position of strength," but teachers also must work actively to be receptive to such an "assumption" and such receptivity does not come automatically or easily. In other words, teachers, too, must examine their own literacy stories and their own "passages between language worlds" (Soliday 511). Wendy S. Hesford, in *Framing Identities: Autobiography and the Politics of Pedagogy*, "propose[s] that teachers-researchers, particularly white critical educators, turn the othering gaze on ourselves and envision new ways of speaking and listening that acknowledge cultural differences and work against the historical tendency to situate ourselves at the center" (9). As Hesford points out, "to situate ourselves at the center" perpetuates attitudes that view academic discourse and largely middle-class white ways of knowing as the standard to which all others will be measured and compared and to which those others will be found lacking. Therefore, an essential process is to reflect on our own stories of literacy acquisition. Hesford writes:

> Integrating our self-reflections with cultural, rhetorical, and material analysis, and encouraging our students to do the same, not only will go a long way toward justifying attention to the personal in the classroom but it will also help us move beyond a naïve and reductive identity politics. I suggest that we turn the pedagogical looking glass upon ourselves and that we use the knowledge gained from critical reflexivity to rewrite the stories we tell about ourselves, our students, and our institutions. (155–6)

Obviously, telling our stories is not enough; analyzing our stories for what they reveal and conceal, for intended and unintended interpretations is the key critical move that can help us see beyond the narrow frames of our identities.

Many of our assumptions regarding others' literacy acquisition emerge from our own experiences of learning to read and write. If that learning came easily and pleasurably to us, we may have difficulty understanding or appreciating the efforts made by our students for whom such learning has come less easily or who have had much less immersion in literacy practices. For example, a former student called recently, in tears, to ask me what to do; a colleague of mine had recommended—on the basis of the difficulties the student had encountered with *Beowulf, The Canterbury Tales*, and other early British texts— that she give up her plan to teach high school English and, instead, switch to a specialization in special education. The student comes from a family and background in which the practices needed to read and make sense with facility of texts written in Middle English or Shakespearean English do not play much of a role, and, even though this class was her first attempt to work through such language, she had earned a *C*. The teacher, from an elite background and education, lacked awareness that some students may require greater efforts—and more time—to be able to work with such specialized language, and were she to consider the privilege and uncommon nature of her own literacy acquisition (that is, turn the "othering gaze" on herself) rather than focusing on the student's perceived linguistic weakness, she could begin to gain such awareness.

As a teacher trainer, I endeavor to see that the teaching assistants I train have opportunities to reflect on their own literacy experiences and literate practices, asking them to write short literacy narratives and to consider what has made them want to teach. The students to whose work I refer in the following text were responding to an assignment in English 675—Colloquium: Teaching Freshman Rhetoric, or as it is commonly known in my department, the teaching colloquium, during the fall 2003 semester. I asked that they write a brief, two- to three-page narrative telling a story about learning to read and write and that, as part of their narrative, they consider where their desire to become highly literate—after all, they are all pursuing advanced degrees in English—came from. Not surprisingly, most come easily to reading and writing, nurtured by parents who encouraged their efforts or by teachers who recognized their gifts. Many, also not surprisingly, represent literacy metaphorically as escape: escape from being an outcast at school, from a neglectful mother, from school tension and violence centering on busing and racial discord. The few who remember learning to read credit their parents' examples (especially their mothers) and recall seeing a mother or father absorbed in a novel or the newspaper. But most describe themselves as "always" knowing how to read. As Scott Lancaster writes, "I don't remember when I learned to read—I feel like reading has always been a part of my life." Again, not surprisingly, no one recalls struggling or having any difficulty whatsoever as they learned to read and write, but noting the factors they see as contributing to that facility with language is interesting. Connie Meyer, for instance, cites a lifelong desire to know about the world: "The driving force behind my life's odyssey in reference to developing my reading and writing skills can be summed up in one word: curiosity, more eloquently termed a 'thirst for knowledge.'" Terry Peterman describes his need "to search to find my faith, and to find my own personal relationship with God" as the source of his drive to be increasingly literate. Paul Mooney writes that reading "was always just there" and sees his ability as a "God-given talent." Significantly these writers (as well as others in the class) see their literacy skills as innate, natural, "just there." Their love of reading and writing has no originary moments.

What they identify as their early learning happens largely by example—a father studying thick books in medical school and a mother weekly borrowing books from the public library. Teachers from school are described largely in terms of recognizing and encouraging talent already in place rather than providing actual instruction. Other teachers are described as hindering rather than helping via strict adherence to rules, lists, or formulas. The questions I ask repeatedly, then, are: How do we teach higher literacy to those for whom the acquisition has been less "natural" and less easily achieved? How do we work with the students who do not share our "curiosity" or our "need to search"? Or if the "talent" is "God-given," why even try to teach those who are not

"God's chosen"? Obviously, I am not expecting simple answers; rather, these are questions for ongoing reflection and consideration, questions designed to get teaching assistants to turn the "othering gaze" on themselves to examine the assumptions that underlie their understanding of the process of learning to read and write with facility.

In the narratives the writers in my two sections of first-year composition classes produced, also in Fall 2003, the associations with reading and writing were on the whole far less positive. Of these forty-four students, none identified themselves as English majors although about one-third wanted to be coaches or elementary school teachers. Several were music majors, but the majority of these students were hoping for careers in computer science or business. In a decidedly unscientific combination attitude survey and ice breaker, almost one-half said they write only when forced; most of the others said that writing was "okay"; and only one, a song writer, admitted that he loved to write—but, of course, he made clear that he loved to write songs, not "school" writing. As in the teaching colloquium, we began the term in the first-year writing class with an assignment that asked the students to write brief stories of their learning to write. From there, we began to develop their stories into a larger theoretical conversation about literacy acquisition and schooling as they read and worked with a variety of texts including a chapter from Richard Rodriguez's *Hunger of Memory*, Susan Glaspell's "A Jury of Her Peers," an excerpt from Shirley Brice Heath's *Ways with Words*, an excerpt from bell hooks's *Talking Back*, several scholarly articles offering solutions to students' literacy failures, and Michael Radford's film *Il Postino*.

We worked through a sequence of writing assignments designed to complicate and deepen their thinking about what literacy means and what is needed to be "literate" at the university level. One assignment asked them to identify and discuss obstacles to achieving critical literacy; the next asked the students to critique others' solutions and offer their own for students' difficulties with and resistance to more demanding reading and writing, and a later one asked that they develop their own metaphor to describe their attitudes toward their efforts to become literate in the ways that would make their success more likely in their college courses. However, as I read their first responses to the early assignments, I was genuinely surprised to learn to what extent state-mandated testing in the public schools overwhelmed our discussions and dominated their writing. Literacy is for all intents and purposes the tests they took as students in the Texas public school system, which they either did or did not pass. When I asked them to talk of critical literacy or "higher" literacy, they talked of tests—TAAS (Texas Academic Assessment and Skills), TASP (Texas Academic Skills Program), or TAKS (Texas Academic Knowledge and Skills). They are generally angry that so many years of their formal schooling were spent being drilled and trained to take tests that controlled everything and everyone around them. I teach at a university that does not generally attract those students who aced these tests with no trauma or drama. Even many of the students in my honors classes speak or write with bitterness of the power of these tests.

In Texas, of course, high-stakes testing began in earnest under then-Governor George W. Bush's mandate. "'Without testing,' [Bush said], 'reform is a journey without a compass. Without testing, teachers and administrators cannot adjust their methods to meet high goals. Without testing, standards are little more than scraps of paper. Without testing, true competition is impossible. Without testing, parents are left in the dark'" (quoted. in Hillocks 11). Students are tested to move from one grade to the next, to graduate from high school, and to be free of "remediation" once they enter a state college or university. The extent of state testing has increased to the point that students entering our university by 2004 have been tested in all but three years of their twelve years in public school, so perhaps we should not be surprised, then, that testing has come to be inextricably linked to any discussion of literacy education.

In their literacy narratives, some students did describe positive early experiences; Elissa Daniel, for example, described writing a book at age ten, and others recalled Dr. Seuss with pleasure. But many of their narratives quickly turned to focus on testing and testing's failure to measure accurately their abilities. As Mallory Baptiste writes, "Standardized testing has always been a problem for me, because I am not a good test taker. I think these tests do measure accuracy, but they do not tell how smart you are. I took the TASP test twice before I passed, but before I passed I felt stupid." Mark Abelson echoes Baptiste's position but adds a touch of sarcasm:

> Since I had the pleasure of taking the TASP three different times on the account that I missed the writing and math part by a few points each time and each time they would put me in a stupid class that would serve orange juice and donuts every Saturday morning and waste a morning of watching good old fashion [sic] cartoons. I think that most high school students drop out of college, because they weren't prepared because all that they would teach us was what we needed to pass the test.

Baptiste and Abelson were by no means the only students to bring state testing to the center of their literacy narratives and to our discussions of literacy acquisition. Tellingly, rather than narrating stories of success, almost all chose to tell stories of obstacles in the way of their success.

Interestingly, however, what also became clear in their narratives is that the lesson they have internalized from their literacy experiences is that they are ultimately responsible for their own success or failure. Axa Lima, for example, writes:

Let us say you have a piece of paper in front of you and you can use it however you wish. One boy uses it to clean up his spilled juice, another girl turns
the paper into a plane and sends it flying to her friend across the room and
the third boy writes his homework on it and turns it in to the teacher. In a
way literacy is just like that piece of paper. Literacy can give you the ability to
do many things but in the end the decision is up to you and me.

Baptiste, after spending considerable time in her essay describing the trauma
of failing the state tests in writing and math twice, claims that the tests
helped her in the long run. She writes that she is determined to succeed,
defining "success" as "[b]eing able to strive for success no matter what you
may lose, types of tests you may have to pass, gender, cultural balance, and
family pressures. . . . Realizing that you have a voice and having motivation,
is the ultimate way to gaining success." As the daughter of an immigrant from
the Virgin Islands, Baptiste writes of her growing awareness of and pride in
her family's difference, but she is horrified by the poverty evidenced in the
photographs of her mother's former home. Her mother told her that children
in her native country had no educational opportunities, and Baptiste is deeply
aware of the sacrifices her mother has made for her and how privileged she
is in being able to attend a university at all. Success, therefore, is entirely her
responsibility as she sees it.

Elissa Daniel echoes this position: "I think that success is earning whatever
it is that you want in life." When asked to engage with Richard Rodriguez's
complex and carefully articulated relationship to his acquisition of English and
higher literacy, she relates the flat facts of his experience, quoting carefully, and
asking questions such as, "In the long run he did gain something very valuable
from learning English, but was it worth it?" She backs off from exploring the
possibility that it was not, however and states, "That conclusion is only for him
to decide." Daniel, a successful student who had no trouble with state tests,
is uncomfortable with the ambiguity of Rodriguez's story, as were many of
her classmates. She stated in class discussion that she could not really understand what he was "complaining" about; after all, he is a successful writer. She
expressed frustration over our discussion and declared that she could find no
way to connect with Rodriguez's regrets. He did well in school; he did what he
was supposed to do; success in school guarantees success in life.

Steve Huffer, however, overtly questions the ways success was defined in
his own schooling and particularly questions the focus on tests and test preparation, frustrated over the lockstep approach to learning that the state tests
engender. He tells the story of being excited by being assigned to read Orwell's
1984, but being chastised by his teacher for reading ahead and being forced to
follow rigid formulas to demonstrate his "successful" reading on work sheets
for each chapter. In his essay's conclusion, he writes, "In order to create a more
literate society, tactics like the one my teacher used will do simply the opposite,

especially [with] high school students." Huffer had wanted to write about the book's "clear political and sociological opinions, as well as some of the frightening parallels [with] modern day society," but, instead, he was required to fill out work sheets "in complete sentences." From the first day of class, Huffer was angry about how his schooling, in essence, interfered with his literacy education. He revealed that he had been placed temporarily in special education classes when he started school because he "had a lot of trouble reading and writing." He eventually, however, discovered that reading and writing give him great pleasure, but gives no credit whatsoever to his teachers; he writes, "I feel the method in which I was taught in high school on how to write was and is totally useless. Too many rules and forms on how to 'correctly' write." In his final retrospective essay, Huffer decides that his parents deserve the credit for his love of reading and writing, not his teachers.

In "Writing on the Bias," Linda Brodkey, narrating the story of her own literacy acquisition, writes:

> Over the years, the schools have probably quelled a desire to write in a good many children by subjecting them to ritualized performances of penmanship, spelling, grammar, punctuation, organization, and most recently thinking. Every generation mixes its own nostrums and passes them off as writing. The fetishes may change but not the substitution of some formal ritual performance for writing. (531)

Work sheets, obviously, are nothing new, but the intense emphasis on these tests has profound impact on our students. As many of us attempt to teach in spite of or beyond the limitations of these tests, hearing our students' anger over the relentlessness of the culture of testing, working to help them problematize their definitions of success and continuing to ask questions about the variety of ways that success can be measured are important.

Every year in the teaching colloquium in an assignment a former colleague, Barbara McCarthy, originally conceived, I ask the new teaching and graduate assistants to write a brief paper developing a metaphor for teaching. Much is compressed in the metaphor, and much can be revealed. Bram Dijkstra argues that metaphors "do the dirty work of ideology" and that "they telescope complex ideas into simple imagery and encourage us to see others not as persons but as patterns" (311). If we accept Dijkstra's characterization of metaphors doing ideology's "dirty work," then unpacking the "complex ideas" from the "simple imagery" is vitally important. The teaching assistants' responses consistently prove to be revealing. Responses ranged from teaching is like performance art to teaching is like war. Pursuing each metaphor to its logical conclusion is useful because such pursuit can provide a shortcut to our assumptions about students and teaching, and once we can more fully critique and work with those assumptions, we can more fully understand and develop our teaching philosophies. For instance, with the first example, in our discussion we were able to talk about teaching in terms of performance, art, and audience; we were able to talk about the rhetorical purposes of performance and how they are similar to and different from teaching; we were able to talk about how the goals for performance (applause perhaps) are not identical to the goals for teaching. In other words, unpacking the metaphor enriched and complicated our concepts of teaching. In the second example, we were able to consider the implications of thinking of teaching in terms of such an extreme scenario. Obviously, that particular teaching assistant felt significant anxiety about being in front of the classroom. In his first semester of teaching, he had experienced resistance and some overt hostility from a few of his male students and was anxious to establish his authority. Admittedly, he was being a bit flippant in his metaphor paper, but even so it again opened up our discussion to questions of authority and power and acknowledged anxiety as a perfectly understandable and to a certain extent even desirable state. (In fact, I am more concerned when a new teaching assistant claims not to be anxious.)

But if, as Lakoff and Johnson argue, metaphors "play a central role in defining our everyday realities" (3), how we describe our teaching and our students will affect what we do and see; that is, if we describe teaching as war, we are more likely to see our students as the enemy, and we are more likely to describe the classroom in terms of winning and losing. This is an important "reality" that deserves and requires reflection. In addition, asking questions and pushing new teachers to consider the implications of their metaphors (what are the possible roles available to participants in war, what are the possible outcomes, what sorts of classrooms are possible within the terms of this metaphor, and so forth) model the kinds of work they can do with their own students.

In their literacy narratives discussed herein, the new teachers were easily able to describe their own attitudes metaphorically, and their attitudes were uniformly positive, which I expect from people hoping to teach college-level English. I knew, however, that the responses from the first-year students in my writing classes would most likely be much more varied. Near the end of our semester-long emphasis on questions of literacy, much later than in the teaching colloquium, I asked the first-year students to develop metaphors for their understandings of or attitudes toward achieving higher literacy. In previous classes (one of which I discuss in chapter 1), I have used online discussion to get students' quick, impromptu descriptions of their attitudes toward reading and writing. However, I wanted to give students a chance to shape a more considered response to see how those responses might differ or what they might add. To complicate their thinking, I screened Michael Radford's *Il Postino*. Because most of the students in these classes admitted to having done little reading for pleasure, the film allowed them to see a metaphor carried throughout the film in ways they probably would have more difficulty seeing in a written text.

"Reading" *Il Postino* via the metaphor of literacy helps students practice seeing a text—any text—as multivalent as they unpack the different ways literacy figures throughout. On the most basic level, of course, the 1994 film can be seen as the main character's literacy narrative. Mario Ruppolo, the son of a fisherman in a small Italian fishing village, has his life changed by Pablo Neruda, who comes to the village as a political exile from his native Chile. At the beginning of the film, all Mario knows is that he does not want to follow his father to the fishing boats as we observe him reading with longing a postcard from two childhood friends who have emigrated to the United States. He wants something more than the life his father and the others in the village have, but he has no clear sense of what that something more could be. To satisfy his father's demand that he find some means of employment, Mario takes a job as a postman whose only delivery is to Pablo Neruda's mountaintop retreat. Enthralled by the romance of Neruda's life and his reputation as "the poet of love," Mario seeks out Neruda's poetry and becomes increasingly caught up in the beauty of Neruda's work. Slowly, a friendship develops between the two men, and slowly, Neruda teaches Mario how to read and appreciate poetry—in other words, Mario is seduced by higher literacy.

Echoing the metaphorical seduction is Mario's seduction of Beatrice, the beautiful, tough, hard-to-get niece of the widow who owns the village's tavern. Initially Beatrice is contemptuous of Mario, but she is eventually wooed by the poems he gives her, poems he has plagiarized from Neruda. With Neruda's help, Mario wins and marries Beatrice, and under Neruda's influence, he begins to write his own poetry, and he begins to identify himself as a communist. At this point, we are prepared for a happy ending with Mario married to the love of his life, befriended by the Nobel Prize–winning poet and writing his own poetry, but the film overturns our expectations. After Neruda's return to Chile, Mario hears nothing from his friend, and even though he feels disappointment at this neglect, he remains true to both poetry and communism. At a communist rally, Mario is prepared to read his poem, a tribute to Neruda, to the crowd, but a riot breaks out, and Mario is mistakenly killed by the police as he struggles to get to the stage. Captured on tape, what was supposed to be his moment of triumph becomes a recording of his death which the widowed Beatrice plays for Neruda when he finally returns, too late, to see his friend. The film closes with Neruda standing on the beach, staring at the sea.

Despite their initial displeasure at having to read subtitles (an interesting literacy issue in itself) and over the unhappy ending, my students generally liked *Il Postino* a lot. Interpreting it as a love story (Mario, a poor fisherman's son, overcomes all obstacles and wins the woman of his dreams through poetry), they tended to ignore the film's problematic ending unless I called their attention to it. Even when I pushed them to imagine the implications of Mario's death, Neruda's arriving too late, and Beatrice's future as a widowed mother with no literacy skills of her own, they continued to speak and write of the film as a success story.

In their writing assignment, I asked them to explore how the metaphor of seduction is played out in *Il Postino*, to consider in what ways literacy could "seduce" one, and to develop their own metaphors to describe their relationship to literacy. The purpose of the assignment is not to produce film analysis or criticism but to help lead students to a more complex discussion of what they want to achieve in college, how their literate practices probably will have to change, and, ultimately, how changing those practices most likely will change them. Not surprisingly, students struggled with the metaphor of seduction outside the context of sexuality, and many took time to stand back and marvel at the very concept of being "seduced" by a desire to read and write, much less a desire to read and write poetry. For example, Rachel Nichols writes, "For me, literacy is far from seduction. It's like trying to open a locked door with the wrong key." Seeing herself as more like Beatrice's literal-minded aunt than like Mario, Nichols writes:

> Sometimes I can be just like Beatrice's aunt, I don't always see the meaning at first and usually I have to have someone explain what the meaning behind the words is. My key is usually in the wrong shape, and I have to have my friend let me in with their [*sic*] key. I tend to think that being in college is enough, but it still isn't going to guarantee higher literacy for me. It is something I am trying to grasp, but I am going about it slowly, simply because I am not so sure of how important it is to me.

Nichols is like many other students in her assumption that "being in college is enough," that it will automatically make her highly literate, and in a sense, if she is able to keep taking and passing classes, she will become more literate in the process—even highly literate compared to others without that opportunity. But in the process of considering her relationship to literacy, she begins also to consider that such criticality may not be her goal. She contrasts Mario and Beatrice's experiences of being "swept away" by the beauty of poetry to her own experience of being "swept away" by a particular Christian rock song, a song that leads her to wonder about "that day when I would see God for the first time." As a member of a religion that believes in revelation rather than questioning, Nichols is right to take the process of questioning—questioning the questioning, if you will—slowly. As Richard Rodriguez knows, education will change her.

Several students developed metaphors that described literacy as the means to their goals. Yet they remained ambivalent about the work such literacy requires. Evan J. Teer, for instance, struggles to make a connection between

literacy and seduction, and the metaphor he comes up with to describe his
own attitudes toward literacy helps us see why: literacy as a puzzle. Teer writes,
"English, I think, has made literacy puzzling to me. English requires you to
think on higher levels than you normally do and about increasingly harder
material over a period of time. I have a lot of trouble with this subject sometimes." Clearly, Teer has never encountered any subject matter or text in his
English classes that has seduced him. More tellingly, he compares himself to a
character in Mike Judge's 1991 film *Office Space*:

> In this movie, the main character hates his job. He has lost all motivation for
> his job if he ever had any that is. He feels as if he is going nowhere and in the
> end, ends up stealing a lot of money from the company. In the movie, he is
> asked if he has quit his job and he replies, "No, I think I'm just not going to
> go anymore." It is a really funny line in the movie, but it also shows how he
> has lost all interest in his job. He quits caring about his job and simply stops
> going. Sometimes I wonder if this will be my case.

Imagining a description that could be more different than those discussed previously by the teaching assistants produced or in the published narratives discussed in chapters 2 and 3 is difficult. Teer works to figure out what he is doing
for the remaining two pages of his essay. He gamely tries to use the puzzle
metaphor to state positively what he is going through—"You have to put it
together piece by piece"—but his conclusion undermines what little optimism
exists. He writes:

> I want to learn new things and altogether grow as the person I am. But
> sometimes I just cannot get motivated no matter how hard I try. I get to
> thinking about how difficult it is to be truly literate and I sometimes wonder
> if it is actually worth it to me. I have to ask myself if I am just wasting all of
> my time with trying to be literate on a higher level. However, I have to tell
> myself that it is ultimately worth it to me.

Teer is anything but enthusiastic about this process, and he seems to see nothing pleasurable in the process of acquiring higher literacy; he can only hope
"that it is ultimately worth it to me." More powerful than the puzzle metaphor
is his comparison of himself as an essay writer to the movie character who
cannot even muster enough passion for his job to quit it.

　　In his essay "Bitter Medicine Can Cure the Sickness," Sean Kennedy,
too, offers a metaphor that sees literacy as the means (that is, "the cure") that
will enable his eventual success—the elimination of his "sickness," which he
defines as "ignorance and simplicity." He writes, "To me, literacy is like drinking cough syrup. If I have an illness or ailment, I know that I must drink the
medicine; I know in my mind that it will cure me and help me to feel better."
He continues, "However, drinking cough syrup is one of the most unpleasant

experiences I have had; the taste of it is horrible, and it usually makes me feel worse at first." Once more, Kennedy's experience is a far cry from seduction. Like Teer, he reflects on his own lack of intellectual curiosity, "There are some people who love to be intellectuals, to contemplate and question all things, and to express their emotions in such a complex and subtle way. I feel almost guilty that I am not, or do not consider myself to be, one of these people." Kennedy admits that he has "never felt a *desire* for this sort of literacy. Rather, I have always tried to do what was essentially expected of me." Unlike Teer, he does not entertain the idea that he could "just not go anymore." Instead, he recalls an example of taking "bitter medicine" during high school when he accepted a position of some authority that required him to speak in front of an audience. While he hated having to speak publicly, he now knows that he is capable of doing it, and so the "medicine" had beneficial effect.

A quiet student in class, Kennedy worked consistently "to do what was essentially expected of [him]." When the assignment asked him to question those expectations, he worked to question them. At several points in his essay, he mentioned that it is important for him to "think for himself," but he admits:

> I find myself still thinking in terms of what people expect of me. I still feel
> the *need* to go to class and to study because I was, more or less, told to. Even
> now, I do not feel as though I have a choice; I feel as though I must meet the
> expectations that others have of me. This is a side of myself that I do not par-
> ticularly like, one that worries too much about what other people think.

Dismissing what Kennedy is saying as mere cliché would be a mistake. Through *Il Postino*'s representation of Mario and Neruda, he has seen two people willing to risk everything for ideas and the right to communicate those ideas in writing for others to read, and he has begun to consider what "medi-cine" he is willing (and unwilling) to swallow as part of his efforts to appropri-ate academic discourses.

In the teaching colloquium, the teaching assistants and I spend a great deal of time focusing on how to ask questions in the classroom and, more important, how to hear students' responses. In some cases, we need to be aware that a student will not be ready to hear or does not wish to consider some questions or some they may never be willing to consider for that matter. In other words, we need to pay attention to what questions students choose not to pursue. Rodrigo Echeverria in his essay "The Seduction of a Family" appro-priated the metaphor of seduction from the film as his own as he described his family's move from Mexico to Texas. He begins:

> In the beginning of the film *Il Postino*, Mario Ruppolo is holding a postcard
> that his cousin sent him from America. Mario was admiring the beauty of the
> United States and the wealth that could be accomplished and acquired. Like

> Mario, my family and I were seduced to come to America in search of a better
> life. The stories that we heard about America made my family leave everything
> behind. My family wanted more than just a simple life. We wanted freedom,
> wealth, and a new life ("The American Dream," in a nutshell).

As Echeverria makes clear throughout his essay, his family's efforts to succeed are, indeed, a family affair; America seduced the entire family. While his
parents work to make each new opportunity pay off, Echeverria and his sister
work to become completely fluent in English and, now, to graduate from college, and then work to contribute to the family's financial success.

Seduction, as he argues, makes things happen: "Without seduction I do
not think that people would be willing to do the things that they do. Seduction is what causes us, humans, to act and interact in ways that will assure us
that we will get what we want. My family and I were seduced by money and
higher education and literacy." I am reminded of Michel Foucault's discussion
of power in "Truth and Power"; he argues that if power were only oppressive,
it just wouldn't work. Power is also productive. Seduction, too, makes us desire
and feel desired; it makes us want, and wanting makes us work to gain the
object of our desire. For Echeverria, seduction is largely positive, and he shares
little with Richard Rodriguez in regard to literacy and loss. He is not leaving his family behind; his family is moving together in their mission to take
advantage of everything the United States has to offer them. Given all that he
and his family have been through and have achieved, he needs to produce a
success narrative that argues that all the sacrifices and hard work are proving
to be worthwhile. The only moment that might call into question his family's
march to financial success and assimilation into American consumer culture
is his essay's last sentence: "Be careful on how you are seduced and how you
use literacy and education because it may have its drawbacks and cause you
problems like Neruda's exile from Chile and Mario's death." Interestingly, this
is also the one place in Echeverria's essay where he switches to second person. He does not overtly connect the warning with himself or his family; it is
addressed to "you." Yet it still reveals his awareness that literacy and education
can make one ask questions that do not necessarily lead to economic success.
Interestingly, when I invited Echeverria to revise and develop what he had
begun in his essay, he declined although he did extensive revision of much of
the rest of his paper. Also, interestingly, he chose to leave it in and keep it in its
place as the last sentence of his essay when he could easily have just deleted it
as "troublesome." He didn't want to talk about it in any more depth, but he still
wanted it there.

Of course, other students' metaphors were positive as well; not all were
ambivalent or negative (and not all were so interestingly developed). Kim
Pacheco, for instance, compared her growing literacy to "winning the jackpot,"
while Jackie Nenninger compared hers to a balloon. But the great majority of

their metaphors were markedly different from those the new teaching assistants wrote. Although literacy narratives can reveal to us something of our students' histories with literacy education, literacy metaphors can offer us equally revealing pictures of their relationships to the reading and writing we are asking of them. We know from some of the most influential essays in composition studies how evocative and powerful metaphors can be and how just a short turn of phrase can produce a veritable paradigm shift in the ways we understand a concept. Consider, for example, the impact "inventing the university" and "contact zone" have had on the scholarship and conversations in our profession.

In his 1985 article "Inventing the University," David Bartholomae problematized our understanding of "the" writing process and what we ask of students in our first-year writing courses. Introducing his metaphor, he writes:

> Every time a student sits down to write for us, he has to invent the university for the occasion—invent the university, that is, or a branch of it, like history or anthropology or economics or English. The student has to learn to speak our language, to speak as we do, to try on the peculiar ways of knowing, selecting, evaluating, reporting, concluding, and arguing that define the discourse of our community. (589)

Bartholomae accomplishes several things in this introduction. First, he reminds us that many students enter college unaware of what to expect or what precisely they will be doing. Second, he questions our assumptions, particularly in 1985, that learning to write is a one-size-fits-all, unitary process. Third, he points out that academic writing is not a unitary discourse but comprises many discourses, that is, the discursive practices I am operating within as I write this would not be acceptable to my colleagues in chemistry. And, most important, he refers to these specialized ways of using language as "peculiar." In a sense, Bartholomae operates as a participant-observer producing a sort of ethnography that turns attention to his own culture and reveals its practices to itself—as if to say look how strange the things we're asking students to do really are. The "ways of knowing" of each discipline are "peculiar" in that what counts as knowledge and how that knowledge is demonstrated differs dramatically from one field of study to another, but more significantly, none of those "ways of knowing" are essential or natural—they, too, were "invented." In slow, careful readings of students' placement essays, he is able to reveal each student's "invention" of the university as it unfolds, that is, through close readings he shows how the student attempts to make sense of and respond appropriately to the writing prompt by attempting to write from a position of authority for an academic audience, an academic audience empowered to determine with what writing course she will begin and, not incidentally, how many courses she will be required to take to pass the university's writing requirement.

But Bartholomae also problematizes teachers' assumptions about what we mean when we instruct students to write for a "specific" audience. Most composition textbooks and writing prompts urge students to work from a clear sense of for whom they are writing when, almost always, the real "specific" audience is the teacher. Bartholomae, however, argues that, even if he were to ask his class to write specifically to and for him, those students are still at a significant disadvantage:

> If my students are going to write for me by knowing who I am—and if this means more than knowing my prejudices, psyching me out—it means knowing what I know; it means having the knowledge of a professor of English. They have, then, to know what I know and how I know what I know (the interpretive schemes that define the way I work out the problems I set for them); they have to learn to write what I would write or to offer up some approximation of that discourse. The problem of audience awareness, then, is a problem of power and finesse. (594–95)

Simplistically, we could say that the student has to invent the professor as well as the university, but that does not describe the magnitude of what the student faces either. The reality is that for students to succeed at the writing task being assigned, they must not only appropriate the discourse, but also the power to speak within that discourse, in other words, "a problem of power and finesse."

Near the end of his article, Bartholomae, drawing from the student texts he includes and addresses, points us to stages generally present in students' efforts to appropriate a discourse: "At the first level, then," he writes, "a student might establish his authority by simply stating his own presence within the field of a subject" (611); that is, the student will tell a first-person story that falls within the topic of the prompt with little or no attempt to draw connections for the reader. The next level is marked by a student's efforts to imitate the forms and characteristic language of a discourse with little substance and, still, little understanding of the function of that discourse. But students can be said to be at an "advanced" stage when they begin to use the discourse itself to assume authority, not to mimic its turns of phrase or methods of organization, but to "plac[e] themselves both within and against a discourse, or within or against competing discourses, and working self-consciously to claim an interpretive project of their own, one that grants them the privilege to speak" (612). One of Bartholomae's real contributions here is to accord to student writing the same respect and attention we accord professional writing. In this way, we can see something of what a close reading of students' texts reveals about how students find places for themselves within a discourse. All of this is packed within the metaphor "inventing the university."

Joseph Harris, however, considers how some metaphors can serve to conceal assumptions as he argues in his Braddock Award–winning article "The Idea of Community in the Study of Writing." The concept of "community" serves a metaphorical function in that it "plays a central role in defining our everyday realities" (Lakoff and Johnson 3). Harris begins his article with a reference to Raymond Williams's book *The Country and the City*, the title of which serves as the operant metaphor for Williams's life. The phrase has its literal origins in Williams's move from his childhood in a Wales village to his adult life in Cambridge, but, of course, the metaphor operates on several levels in that it also refers to the sense of dislocation one feels in such a transition and to the fact that, as Harris puts it, "one only begins to understand the place one comes from by leaving it" (260). Williams's metaphor resonates for Harris as he draws from his own move from a working-class background into academia and the resulting sense of never again fully belonging to either: "This sense of difference, of overlap, of tense plurality, of being at once part of several communities and yet never wholly a member of one, has accompanied nearly all the work and study I have done at the university" (260). "This sense of difference" enables him to be aware of and be suspicious of attempts to describe academia in unifying terms that are blind to or denigrate difference. His purpose is to problematize one such unifying term—the concept of community as he sees it invoked in composition studies, particularly by Bartholomae and Patricia Bizzell.

Harris clearly admires Bartholomae and Bizzell's body of work, especially for their success in broadening the field's focus to include "the power of social forces in writing" as well as "the composing processes of individual writers" (261). But such broadening can become, in some respects, too broad, as in the uncritical invocation of a "discourse community" or "academic community" which, as Williams's discussion in *Keywords* reveals, is never used in any but a positive sense and thus can become "an empty and sentimental word" (262). Harris shows how "community" functions in Bartholomae's article "Inventing the University" as "a kind of stabilizing term, used to give a sense of shared purpose and effort to our dealings with the various discourses that make up the university" (263). But who is this "we" to which Bartholomae refers, asks Harris. This use of the first person plural is vague, as is the use of the phrase "discourse community." Again, the reference to Williams and "the country and the city" as well as Harris's own sense of being simultaneously an academic insider and outsider disrupt the seeming seamlessness of these metaphors:

> Rather than doing much the same, romanticizing academic discourse as occurring in a kind of single cohesive community, I would urge, instead, that we think of it as taking place in something more like a city. That is, instead of presenting academic discourse as coherent and well-defined, we might be better off viewing it as a polyglot, as a sort of space in which competing beliefs and practices intersect with and confront one another. One does not need consensus to have community. Matters of accident, necessity, and convenience hold groups together as well. (268–69)

Certainly, the students who populate a typical writing class—at least where I teach—can be said to have come together via "accident, necessity, and convenience." "Academic discourse" has served as an enabling fiction as I work to convince these students not only to write beyond the five-paragraph formula and to see themselves as writers, but also to help them understand that how they write in English 101 will not be directly transferable to Biology 101. Particularly in a college or university setting where a great many students are first-generation college students, "academic discourse" itself can be seen as a metaphor for these ways of speaking and writing that may be unfamiliar, but the term should not be taken as a literal naming of these ways of speaking and writing under one umbrella term.

Metaphors do important intellectual work, but Harris shows us how necessary pushing back at them is to see in what ways they can do unintended work as well. This is the gist of my own argument: interrogating our own metaphors for what we do—regardless what side of the class roster we are on—to determine whether unquestioned assumptions may be having the opposite effects of those we intend is important. Recall the difference between describing teaching as performance art or war. So the metaphors we take up with particular enthusiasm are worth close and careful examination.

Harris's description of academic discourse as "a sort of space in which competing beliefs and practices intersect with and confront one another" is remarkably similar to Mary Louise Pratt's concept of the "contact zone," another metaphor widely embraced within composition studies. Pratt's "Arts of the Contact Zone" argued, among other things, that the contact zone metaphor can be used "to reconsider the models of community that many of us rely on in teaching and theorizing and that are under challenge today" (530). Pratt begins her article, originally presented as the keynote address at the second Modern Language Association's Literacy Conference in 1990, with two seemingly disparate examples—her son's passion for baseball cards and statistics as a powerful introduction to literacy, and a seventeenth-century 1,200-page letter from Peruvian Guaman Poma to King Philip III of Spain. Poma's *The First New Chronicle and Good Government* informs the king of the acts—some of them unspeakable atrocities—being done in his name as part of the Spanish conquest of South America. Yet Poma was not in any kind of official position to produce such a document, and it remained virtually unread and unreadable until the 1970s "as positivist reading habits gave way to interpretive studies and colonial elitisms to postcolonial pluralisms" (530). Poma's text—its history and context—leads Pratt to the concept of the "contact zone," which she defines as "social spaces where cultures meet, clash, and grapple with each other, often in contexts of highly asymmetrical relations of power, such as colonialism, slavery, or their aftermaths as they are lived out in many parts of the world today" (530). In other words, the contact zone is a site where cultures meet on not necessarily equal terms and where power is negotiated, not necessarily fairly.

Pratt describes Poma's *New Chronicle* as an "autoethnographic text," which means that he is attempting to explain himself and his culture to others who are in positions of power and who hold a perception of his culture that justifies, as far as the Spanish are concerned, its subjugation. Yet who is Poma to attempt to communicate with a king? His use of Spanish is crude, and he is not of high noble birth. He is not in a position to be heard, and, therefore, he is not heard. As Pratt explains:

> Autoethnography, transculturation, critique, collaboration, bilingualism, mediation, parody, denunciation, imaginary dialogue, vernacular expression—these are some of the literate arts of the contact zone. Miscomprehension, incomprehension, dead letters, unread masterpieces, absolute heterogeneity of meaning—these are some of the perils of writing in the contact zone. (536)

Pratt's son Manuel encounters these "perils" on a small scale when his teacher either cannot hear or refuses to acknowledge his parodic voice in a homework response that argues for a shot to make school unnecessary—that is, he is arguing to be inoculated against school. Poma's audience cannot hear—or has too much invested in not hearing—his descriptions of and arguments against Spanish colonial rule. Manuel's teacher either cannot imagine parody as a response or has no time to respond to what his or her students are saying. In both cases, writing in the contact zone has not produced evidence that either writer has been comprehended—or, perhaps, even been read at all.

Where is the "discourse community" for either of these writers? Obviously for both the playing field is not equal. As Pratt points out, "Teacher-pupil language . . . tends to be described almost entirely from the point of view of the teacher and teaching, not from the point of view of pupils and pupiling (the word doesn't even exist, though the thing certainly does)" (538). What needs to be done to provide the pupils' point of view? It seems to me that one move is to respect their representations of their experiences—even when that representation is counter to or resistant to what we expect or what we want to hear. Consider Evan J. Teer's essay "Literacy as a Puzzle" quoted earlier; his reference to *Office Space* certainly was not one I wanted to hear (more likely, the savvier student would have offered some comment that said something flattering about how this English class was challenging him in new and important ways or something similar), but the reference is one I needed to hear. I cannot assume that my students are motivated by the same things I am motivated by or desire the same things I desire, nor should I. I also do not want to "hustle" Teer, to sell him something he genuinely does not want, something that has the potential to separate him from family and friends, as

Richard Rodriguez's—as well as my own—experience shows us. Similarly, I would be out of line to demand that Rodrigo Echeverria overtly critique his family's desire and quest for financial security.

At the same time, in writing their metaphors in some detail, both have the chance to hear their own answers to these questions. That is not to say that they have worked out everything to neat conclusions by the end of their essays, or even by the end of the semester, but the questions have been asked and they have begun to find answers. Pratt concludes her essay with a call for a continuing search "for the pedagogical arts of the contact zone":

> These will include, we are sure, exercises in storytelling and in identifying with the ideas, interests, histories, and attitudes of others; experiments in transculturation and collaborative work and in the arts of critique, parody, and comparison (including unseemly comparisons between elite and vernacular cultural forms); the redemption of the oral; ways for people to engage with suppressed aspects of history (including their own histories), ways to move *into and out of* rhetorics of authenticity; ground rules for communication across lines of difference and hierarchy that go beyond politeness but maintain mutual respect; a systematic approach to the all-important concept of *cultural mediation*. (541; author's italics)

Much is packed in this long sentence, much that is exciting, but she also leaves the door open to critique in her romanticization of the contact zone because the playing field is even more uneven than she describes.

How does a teacher maintain "mutual respect" where the power differential is great as in, for example, a class I observed several years ago. The sequence of reading and writing assignments included a column originally written in the *Chronicle of Higher Education* by a woman who was struggling through graduate school to earn her doctorate degree while receiving government assistance. The teaching assistant struggled to keep the class focused on the text, but several vocal students kept returning to their anger over and frustration with what they understood the welfare system to be. One young woman cited a "welfare family" in her small town that had "one baby after another" so they could get more and more "welfare money." Other class members offered examples that echoed these assumptions, assumptions claiming that all people on welfare are lazy and do not want to work. When the teaching assistant attempted to use the reading's author as a means to counter their characterizations, she inadvertently tapped another source of anger—that their taxes were paying for the writer's education. At our university most students work, many working long hours and commuting long distances to afford and attend college. That the writer was using the welfare system to support herself and her children while she earned an advanced degree enraged several of the students, and the discussion became even more heated. In our postobservation meeting, the teaching assistant expressed surprise that one of the students in the class had remained silent throughout the discussion because she knew the student was currently receiving government assistance and had been for some time. She kept hoping the student would step in and help her classmates gain a more balanced perspective.

Yet who would not maintain silence in such a context and in the face of such anger and frustration? And simply to provide facts and information to demonstrate to students the errors in their assumptions would most likely not sway them in any significant way. Their anger was complex. Guaman Poma's informational (and long) *New Chronicle* failed to have any effect on the Spanish conquistadors and priests—indeed, it was not even read—because the conquest was a part of a process of their belief system, their entire way of perceiving themselves and the world. The same can be said, in a certain sense, about the students in the class just discussed. To think of the angry students as "ignorant Texas rednecks" serves no productive purpose and ignores the circumstances that many of them come from. About one-half of our students are first-generation college students, and many come from families who live from paycheck to paycheck. In fact, many are probably one or two missed paychecks away from government assistance themselves, so, keenly aware of their own financial sacrifices and hardships, they are less than sympathetic—the example of the "welfare mother" cuts too close to the bone. Pratt's argument that, in the contact zone "[t]he sufferings and revelations were, at different moments to be sure, experienced by every student" simply does not always hold true.

Richard E. Miller describes this gap as "fault lines," and his article "Fault Lines in the Contact Zone" tests the limits of Pratt's metaphor as he offers the example of a student-written essay describing a gay bashing that may or may not have happened. "Queers, Bums, and Magic" is truly oppositional discourse, discourse guaranteed to offend any and all writing teachers. Miller describes the array of responses at a session at the Conference on College Composition and Communication where the writer's teacher used the essay to talk about the limits of our vocabulary in responding to student writing. I, too, attended that session and can recall audience members arguing for every possible response from awarding the paper an *F* for not meeting the assignment's guidelines to recommending psychiatric treatment and a call to the police. But Miller argues that "adopting any classroom strategy that isolates this essay and treats it as an anomaly misreads both the essay's cultural significance and its pedagogical possibilities" (396–97). He continues:

> If we step back from "Queers, Bums, and Magic" for a moment and consider the fact that the mixture of anger, rage, ignorance, and confusion that produced this student essay are present in varying degrees on college campuses across the country, what is truly significant about this event is not that it occurred, but that it occurs so rarely. This, surely, is a testament to the

immense pressures exerted by the classroom environment, the presentation of the assigned readings, the directions included in the writing assignments, and the range of teaching practices which work together to ensure that conflicts about or contacts between fundamental beliefs and prejudices do not arise. (398–99)

In other words, we generally orchestrate our classes so that we control what little contact occurs in the contact zone so we can end the class believing "civil discourse" has "opened" our students' minds. But, as Miller writes, "Required self-reflexivity does not, of course, guarantee that repugnant positions will be abandoned" (407). Again, like Guaman Poma, we assume "rationality" will win the day and that people will understand the illogic of their prejudices, but most of the time, our letters go unread, our arguments fail to convince.

Of course, one problem is that we assume that we know what our students believe and think. When I was teaching at another university, I observed a first-year writing teacher begin his class by asking students to identify "typical" traits of men and women. His plan was to list their responses on the board and, ultimately, reveal the students' sexism to them in a triumphant final moment. His students, however, immediately saw through his plan and protested that they could not possibly list "typical" traits because so many ways exist to be a man or a woman. They overturned the class plan entirely and ended up making the teacher appear sexist in his even asking such a question. He was so taken by surprise (and had prepared no backup plan), he dismissed his class early. Does this mean that no sexism existed in his class in any form? Certainly not. It means that the students were savvy to "the immense pressures exerted by the classroom environment" (398). It also means that they were able to read the teacher's prejudices; that is, they were able to read his assumptions about them. A former student described a capstone course on cultural diversity thusly: "The teacher gives us a topic, we yell at each other until somebody cries, then she lets us go." The teacher, no doubt, would be appalled to hear her course described in this way; she, no doubt, believes that she is helping students recognize and transcend their prejudices.

But generally our students are able to read us well and know what will please us as well as what will agitate us, and just because our students do not write an essay such as "Queers, Bums, and Magic" in our classes does not mean they cannot. This past semester, several students in one class resisted the meta-phor assignment. We discussed their resistance, and one student's response was that it was "too gay" to write metaphors. Our subsequent discussion revealed very real evidence of homophobia—which did not shock me, but I asked them to help me understand how they were using the word, what they understand it to mean. Homophobic stereotypes and fears emerged, despite their repeated assurances that using the term did not mean they hated anybody. I let them know that it "worried" me in that I just did not see "gay" as a pejorative, which opened the door for other students to step in to represent other positions, always being careful not to chastize anyone for not seeing things my way. Of course, I knew I would not change any minds if I lectured them on how wrong they were; additionally, I was able to keep the discussion alive, returning to it several times during the semester, each time emerging from our discussion in interesting ways. I could, in fact, see some of the students working through some of their assumptions about sexuality, not surprising in a group composed largely (although not entirely) of eighteen-year-olds. I am not claiming any dramatic breakthroughs or revelatory moments; I just wanted to keep the conversation going to keep alive the possibility of thinking and learning.

The challenge, then, is to find within the contact zone productive ways to work and negotiate that do not set up students to look like chumps, louts, or dopes and that make real, intellectual work possible. Miller writes:

> In the uncharted realms of teaching and studying in the contact zone, the teacher's traditional claim to authority is thus constantly undermined and reconfigured which, in turn, enables the real work of learning to negotiate and to place oneself in dialogue with different ways of knowing how to commence. This can be strangely disorienting work, requiring, as it does, the recognition that in many places what passes as reason or rationality in the academy functions not as something separate from rhetoric, but rather as one of many rhetorical devices. (*Fault* 407)

Once we conceive of the classroom in terms of "social spaces where cultures meet, clash, and grapple with each other" (Pratt 530), we enter "uncharted territory" where we both "grapple" and are "grappled with." In other words, we have to train ourselves to a certain kind of flexibility that enables us to forego shock or anger in favor of the "real work" of negotiation and dialogue. What do the students in our classes have to say to us? What can they teach us? What is the "logic" of their positions? How do we respond in ways that do not just shut them up or shut them down but, instead, invite a continuing dialogue?

At the conclusion of "The Idea of Community in the Study of Writing," Joseph Harris writes, "As teachers and theorists of writing, we need a vocabulary that will allow us to talk about certain forces as social rather than communal, as involving power but not always consent. Such talk could give us a fuller picture of the lived experience of teaching, learning, and writing in a university today" (269–70). I agree that a need for such a vocabulary exists, but we can produce it organically within each class as part of, in Richard Miller's terms, "the real work of learning to negotiate and to place oneself in dialogue with dialogue with different ways of knowing how to commence" (407). For example, "too gay" became part of an ongoing dialogue on several levels; in our dialogues we were able to consider the power of language to communicate, exclude, and do damage; we were able to broach the topic of sexuality and consider why students in their first semester of their first year of college might be nervous about sexuality and talking about sexuality; and we were able to consider intentions and how language is not entirely in the control of the speaker or writer, that is, that the speaker did not mean "too gay" to be offensive did not matter; the audience could still be offended. So, too, "office space" became a metaphor for just putting in one's time at a job and for their fear that an unrewarding cubicle job awaits them; it opened up "space" for us to talk about the nature of higher education both culturally and personally.

When I refer to "the personal" in my writing classes, I am calling neither for a return to expressivist methods whereby students write to "discover" their "true" selves nor to current-traditional methods that place personal writing at the beginning of a modal approach because it is presumed to be the "easiest" place to begin. Students need to have a "personal" connection to what they are writing, reading, and thinking about, however, to feel invested in the work we do in our classes. As I contend in my introduction, the desire to pursue a topic—to do research in any real sense—springs from "personal" interest. I am personally interested in the research I am doing here because it springs from my desire to make sense of my own lifelong drive for higher literacy, a drive that makes no sense given my class and family background. Additionally, we can derive real pleasure relating and connecting to personal experience, pleasure we need not deny ourselves or our students.

The "personal" has garnered enough recent attention in the profession that *College English* published two special issues on the topic, one in September 2001 and another in September 2003 with Jane E. Hindman serving as special editor for both. A symposium collective on "The Politics of the Personal: Storying Our Lives against the Grain" (Brandt et al.) begins the discussion in the 2001 issue with special focus on teachers' dilemmas in using narrative and in drawing from the personal in their research. In "Protecting the Personal," Deborah Brandt, for example, finds that the personal stories of the people she interviews in her research can distract readers from the theory the stories support. Anne Ruggles Gere writes of her conscious efforts to keep her faith strictly separate from her research. After describing her coming out as a lesbian in her contribution to *Comp Tales*, Anne Herrington in "When Is My Business Your Business?" on the other hand, argues that "[p]ersonal narrative does not have a special purchase on insight or knowledge" although we should consciously work to consider "the personal" and "decide for ourselves whether and how to include it in our public writing, whatever the genre" (49). What all eight participants in the collective share is an acute awareness of, in Gesa Kirsch's words in "Negotiating the Personal, the Private, and the Professional":

> the tensions surrounding the personal, the private, and the professional: the
> desire to reveal and the desire to conceal, the difficulty of integrating the

personal and professional dimensions of one's life. . . . Only by making visible these tensions can we hope to change academic cultures and institutions (institutions that seem to have an inordinate ability to absorb—rather than respond to challenges) and to change the personal, the private, and the professional dimensions in our lives. (57)

Kirsch argues that the critical and strategic use of the personal has at least the potential to help effect social change. Taking the personal seriously opens up social spaces to begin to question institutional "of course's" that have real power over our lives. The act of coming out, for example, remains an act of real courage and optimism in many parts of the country and on many campuses, but as Richard Miller states in "Why Bother with Writing?" as part of the symposium collective:

> The predictable states of nervousness that are produced when one speaks of hope in an academic context particularly warrant attention, I would argue, because these states give us direct access to the ways in which what is felt internally as "personal experience" is intimately connected to the institutions outside the self that foster and promote such feelings. (50)

In other words, what we experience as "personal" is not separate from the professional—or the impersonal—but is utterly imbricated in it and with it.

Of course, as Kirsch shows, the question arises about what we do with others' personal experience. How can we respond in any way other than with a nod of recognition, a shrug of boredom, or a gasp of shock? And in our classrooms how do we evaluate our students' written use of the personal? Candace Spigelman's "Argument and Evidence in the Case of the Personal," the first full article in the 2001 special issue, argues that personal experience not only can serve the purpose of academic writing, but also that it "serves the *same* purposes of academic writing and that narratives of personal experience can accomplish serious scholarly work" (64, author's italics). She continues, "I want to move beyond the notion of the personal as supplement to advance the position that narrative, in its various forms, is a logical and legitimate mode of argument appropriate to the academic writing of both composition scholars and their students" (64). Drawing from Aristotle, she goes on to argue for the need for rules to delineate appropriate use of the personal from spurious, manipulative use. Spigelman offers a brief history of the debate of the legitimacy and appropriateness of personal narrative in academic settings and remarks that "the question of the personal in composition remains stunningly political" (69) and, in particular, targets teachers who reserve the right to write in first person for themselves but not for their students. Comparing two published examples of personal narrative written to advance an argument about how teachers should respond to their students' writing, Spigelman demonstrates the need to question authorial assumptions to evaluate the argument:

> While it is true, as critics have argued, that we cannot judge the truth of a
> writer's sense of his or her own lived experience (we cannot say that an event
> did not happen in a particular way if the speaker says that it did), we can
> nevertheless evaluate his or her interpretation of narrative events for their
> fidelity by examining his or her assumptions. (81)

This strikes me as a particularly useful way to approach and interrogate our
own and our students' personal writing and is precisely how I ask both teaching assistants and first-year writing students to approach their literacy narratives. A heart-warming story of learning to read in Grandma's lap is not
enough in itself; we need to look beyond the "seduction" of the story to the
arguments and assumptions being made about literacy acquisition. When
teaching assistant Mike Marlowe describes his desire to read and write in the
terms of "escape" and offers a narrative of being an outcast in school, one can
legitimately ask what the argument being made about literacy is and easily
move to ask the implications of such a narrative for teaching.

Furthermore, because "we cannot judge the truth of a writer's sense of
his or her own lived experience" (Spigelman 81) students are able to speak
with authority about that experience—especially students from traditionally
marginalized groups. Certainly a narrative of an event is not enough in itself;
our work is to enable students to use their narratives to move toward and make
larger arguments; our work is to recognize and read those arguments. I am
reminded of Guaman Poma's letter narrating atrocities to the Spanish king; it
probably was not the narrative the Spanish could not read; it was Poma's argument about the immorality of those atrocities that was illegible to them.

In "Written through the Body," an article in the second special edition of
College English titled "The Personal in Academic Writing," William Banks:

> foreground[s] teaching and writing as embodied (that is, gendered, sexual-
> ized) practices that contain within them markers of identity that require us
> to revisit our pasts or which . . . can subject us to shame. Underneath it all, I
> want to highlight the transformative potential such teaching and writing can
> have. ("Written" 22)

In other words, Banks calls for us to use narrative to examine critically those
moments when we are most "embodied," moments when we are, perhaps, at
our most vulnerable. Although I would add *classed* to his definition of *embodied*, I agree that teachers, in particular because of our complicated positions
of authority, have a responsibility to be self-reflexive and work to be continu-
ally conscious of the ways our own "embodiedness" figures in the teaching and
evaluating of students. Banks, exploring the genre of creative nonfiction, inter-
sperses his article with five "figures" that offer narrative snapshots, narrative
moments that enact his definition of embodiment and enact his argument:

"My signposts (divorce, denial, [dis]location, separation, [re]location) represent one path I've cut through English studies and academia" (37). Ultimately, he argues for English as "an *ethical* discipline, one concerned with the *ethos* of the writer," and, as such, those of us teaching within the discipline:

> should think carefully before exiling "personal" writing, for such writing, more so than any other format I can think of, offers us and our students spaces to think through all those multiple and shifting signifiers at work on us so that we come up with sharper understandings of ourselves and those around us. (38, author's italics)

Here is expressivism (that is, writing to "come up with sharper understandings of ourselves and those around us") but with a twist, a twist that presumes ethics and the political (and personal) implications of ethical action. Therefore, the story near the beginning of this chapter of the professor recommending special education as a new teaching field to her working-class student is not an innocent story. What we "embody" or fail to embody or fail to recognize as "embodied" in others has real effect. What "figure," what narrative snapshot, might this teacher describe to reflect on that effect?

At the very end of *Metaphors We Live By*, Lakoff and Johnson write:

> . . . metaphors are not merely things to be seen beyond. In fact, one can see beyond them only by using other metaphors. It is as though the ability to comprehend experience through metaphor were a sense, like seeing or touching or hearing, with metaphors providing the only ways to perceive and experience much of the world. Metaphor is as much a part of our functioning as our sense of touch, and as precious. (239)

According to Lakoff and Johnson, we "understand and experience one kind of thing in terms of another" (5). In other words, metaphors operate at the center of our ability to make sense of the world around us, from the big questions to the small moments. To make sense of others' metaphors, however, we require contexts—the kind of context narrative can provide. So metaphors for literacy are enriched by being read alongside literacy narratives and can assist both teacher and student in their efforts to make connections to learning and to each other.

I'll conclude by returning to *Oleanna*. In the play's first act, Carol, in desperation, comes to John to make sense of her failing grade. How could she be failing? She's a good student. A scholarship student. But John talks over her, interrupts her, and assumes he knows what she is going to say before she says it. Yes, she is the perfect representation of the student we generally hate to deal with, the student who says, "Just tell me what you want," the student who just does not get it and refuses to pretend that she does, the student who is frustrated and frustrating. Even when John decides to be Super Teacher and work with her individually outside of class and bend rules for her, he still is not hearing what her concerns are; he is, instead, pasting his own experience of failure over hers. By the final two acts, we see evidence of Carol's learning as she becomes increasingly articulate and professional. But John can be said only to have taught her in an odd perversion of teaching. That is, we can say she has learned at John's expense rather than from his classroom teaching or private "tutorial" as Carol, taking everything he has said in the strictest literal sense, charges him with sexual harassment and, ultimately, rape. I offer this not as a cautionary tale that warns teachers to keep their doors open and look out or they, too, will be brought up on questionable charges. Rather, I wish to show that teaching and learning happen whether we necessarily intend them. In Carol's case, her "group" filled the gap John's blindnesses and failures left. If we fail to find ways to enable our students to connect personally as well as intellectually with what we are asking of them—and to hear how and when learning is and is not taking place—their learning, too, will take place elsewhere.

Chapter Five

On the Bias

Literacies, Lived, Written, and Owned

At the recent Conference on College Composition and Communication, I told a former graduate school classmate about writing this book and how I was trying to make sense of a passion for literacy among people like us. Several of us in our graduate program, children of working-class parents, considerably older than our middle-class peers, were struggling to earn enough money to live on at the same time we were struggling to earn our doctorate degrees. "Where did this passion come from?" I asked her. Her response: "Alienation." *GOOD ANSWER*

This chapter details several working-class literacy narratives—some are academic memoirs, some are celebrations of reading and much-loved books—to see how these published, successful writers describe their relationship to literacy. I look at literacy narratives avid, passionate readers and writers composed, readers and writers Heath or Lareau did not anticipate, readers and writers whose passion for literacy defies prediction. My inclusion of these particular narratives is more a result of random selection than an attempt to offer a definitive picture of "the working-class literacy narrative." The questions I ask of these particular narratives could be asked of any literacy narrative, questions such as: What can we learn about teaching from these writers? What role do schools play in their learning? What can we take from these representations of literacy acquisition and the desire for higher literacy into our classrooms? Or is this desire something innate that cannot be taught—they either have it or they do not? Do students have to come to our classrooms already passionate? — *no.*

As Jerome Bruner writes, "It is through our own narratives that we principally construct a version of ourselves in the world, and it is through its narrative that a culture provides models of identity and agency to its members" (xiv). But, certainly, questions of identity are complicated. Who is this self constructing the narrative? And the narrative itself lends itself to a modernist definition of a unitary self. As Lester Faigley points out in *Fragments of Rationality: Postmodernity and the Subject of Composition*:

> Where composition studies have proven least receptive to postmodern theory is in surrendering its belief in the writer as an autonomous self. Since the beginning of composition teaching in the late nineteenth century, college writing teachers have been heavily invested in the stability of the self and the attendant beliefs that writing can be a means of self-discovery and intellectual realization. (15)

Of course the literacy narrative tends toward a representation of a self reaching a level of self-actualization via the writer's relationship with reading and writing. Frederick Douglass's credo could easily be, "I write; therefore, I am." Most literacy narratives, however, do not offer the multivalence or complexity that Douglass offers. Many offer seamless stories of success that reveal little sense of conflict and even less of contradiction. Yet, regardless whether conflict is present, some writers of literacy narratives need to tell stories of their love for books and literacy. For example, individuals whose families shared and supported their passion for literacy from their earliest memories generally tell elite literacy narratives. Usually tending toward the category of the feel-good story, such narratives, such as Anne Fadiman's *Ex Libris*, reveal their writers to be somewhat eccentric compared to others—perhaps even a touch neurotic—in their love for the written word, but happy in their relationship with their books. Fadiman, for instance, describes for our amusement the story of the merging of her library with her husband's well into their marriage. The only "conflict" is deciding whose duplicate copies of which books stay and whose go, as each clings lovingly to well-marked novels from long past college courses. Jane Tompkins' *A Life in School: What the Teacher Learned*, another "elite" narrative, tells the story of a highly successful life of academic literacy whose only conflict comes near the end as she questions her march to academic success and its subsequent costs.

Novelist Lynne Sharon Schwartz's ironically titled literacy memoir *Ruined by Reading: A Life in Books* offers another story of a middle-class child whose passion for books and reading may strike some as odd but not anomalous. She describes her parents as "people of the book" who encourage her passion for reading, a skill she learned from a neighbor at age three. At age four, she becomes a "prodigy" as her father has her read from the *New York Times* at random to impress guests (18). Reading itself she describes as "magical":

"Because I read when I could still believe in magic, reading was magical, not merely breaking a code or translating one set of symbols into another. The idea of translatability was itself magical, and so it remains" (19). Reading becomes increasingly a major focus for her life. She writes, "It started—my reading—innocently enough, and then it infiltrated. It didn't replace living; it infused it, till the two became inextricable, like molecules of hydrogen and oxygen in a bead of water. To part them could take violent and possibly lethal means, a spiritual electrolysis" (24). In a real sense, one is reminded of the way a lover speaks of the beloved. Schwartz does not, however, claim that reading has the power to make us better people or to offer us models for living, "If no girl was ever ruined by a book, none was ever saved by one either" (114). Nor does she claim that reading turns us into walking encyclopedias, stuffed with knowledge that we can access at a moment's notice. I was, in fact, relieved to learn that she forgets much of what she reads; what matters is the moment of reading, not the recall of reading. She argues that reading offers us something more intimate, more spiritual:

me, too. [margin note]

> If we make books happen, they make us happen as well. Reading teaches receptivity, Keats' negative capability. It teaches us to receive, in stillness and attentiveness, a voice possessed temporarily, on loan. The speaker lends herself and we do the same, a mutual and ephemeral exchange, like love. Yet unlike love, reading is pure activity. It will gain us nothing but enchantment of the heart. And as we grow accustomed to receiving books in stillness and attentiveness, so we can grow to receive the world, also possessed temporarily, also enchanting the heart. (118)

Ultimately, Schwartz sees reading—especially a child's reading—as "an act of reclamation," done wholly for oneself; "[t]his was the way to make my life my own" (119).

Nothing surprises us about Fadiman's, Tompkins's, or Schwartz's tales of literacy acquisition—except, perhaps, the extent of their love of literacy. They are the children of Heath's townspeople or Lareau's middle-class parents whose ways of using language prepare the way for their daughters' successes with reading and writing. But closer consideration of Schwartz's description of reading as "the way to make my life my own" can help us see what motivates some children of the working class, probably without parents working to prepare their way, to desire and acquire higher literacy as well. Drawing from *Women's Ways of Knowing*, Christopher Schroeder in *ReInventing the University: Literacies and Legitimacy in the Postmodern Academy* explores the individual's move from "received knowing" to "constructed literacies." Schroeder builds on categories borrowed from Belenky's, Clinchy's, Goldberger's, and Tarule's research with women subjects to inform his understanding of his own intellectual development. "Received knowing" refers to the individual's acceptance of outside authority as truth. From received knowing, one can move to "pro-cedural knowing," which he defines as "knowing that exchanges a mixture of received and subjective knowledges, with the concomitant problems of author-ity, for a knowing based upon reasoning and reflecting and that recognizes the differences of authority that distinguish between separate and connected knowing" (27). In other words, procedural knowing begins to move away from easy (or grudging) acceptance of authority as the individual begins to appropri-ate "how-to" knowledge, reflect on experience and results, and, thereby, make judgments. Schroeder's final distinction is "constructed knowing": "know-ing that reconciles the authorial differences between separate and connected knowing" (27)—that is, knowing that brings received knowledge, individual experience, and procedural knowledge together. Of course, these categories, or "ways" of knowing, should not be perceived as distinct and concrete, but they help us conceive of what can take place to enable the motivation for critical literacy where such literacy is unexpected. A Mike Rose, for instance, finds his experience not accounted for in what he learns in school, and, for whatever reasons, he asks why. Again, nothing surprises us about Anne Fadiman's move to and desire for higher literacy because she is surrounded by passionately lit-erate people; indeed, we would be surprised if she did not embrace higher lit-eracy. But a Mike Rose has to notice "authorial differences between separate and connected knowing," and, more important, he has to care about and to act on that awareness.

But what brings about this awareness, and what might motivate us to care about it once we notice it? As James Collins and Richard Blot point out in *Literacy and Literacies: Texts, Power, and Identity*, "School is the place where social class becomes personal," especially for young women. In my own case, I noticed that some people had more money than others, but I remained largely unaware of class distinctions until my family moved to a "nicer" neighborhood where I enrolled in a "better" high school. I had been in honors classes up until then, but at the new school, I was placed in "regular" classes. To my recollec-tion, neither I nor my parents were consulted about the change, nor did it occur to us to protest the switch. Snubs and digs from middle-class classmates were commonplace. I vividly recall a well-dressed young woman picking up my homemade dress as I changed for gym class and sneering to the others in the locker room, "Look, everybody, loving hands at home." Sadly, too, I do not recall one word of encouragement from any of my teachers in any of my classes at that "better" high school. Not surprisingly, perhaps, I dropped out of school before the end of that term. It was only my sophomore year of high school.

Collins and Blot write, "We would be foolhardy to deny the benefits of literacy and education. . . . Nonetheless, schooling is also where lessons are learned about class, gender, and race, where one's self or one's literacy are deemed adequate or inadequate. Put otherwise, school-related categories are available as categories of identity, that is, as forms of self-definition" (98). The writers here emphasize the contradictory nature of public education. On the one hand, no one can argue against the role literacy education plays in our enculturation and in our abilities to survive economically. On the other hand, school can also teach us "our places" within culture, can teach us that we do not belong in honors courses, or that we do not belong, period.

If we were reading about my experiences of high school in Heath's or Lareau's research, we would predict that I would have gone on to struggle economically, working hourly wage jobs, never moving past my parents' socioeconomic position. Because my father dropped out of high school and my mother describes herself as "barely" graduating, assuming that I would continue the same pattern would be logical. Yet I went back and finished at that "better" high school, went to college, and eventually (certainly setting no land-speed records in the process) received my doctorate degree. The lessons that I did not belong did not "stick." I was a passionate reader who felt more at home with books than anywhere else. Perhaps feeling at home in books led me to identify myself as belonging in a world of books somehow, even though the usual reinforcers (family, teachers, peers, and so forth) were absent.

Collins and Blot argue that identity is, in fact, a complex, complicated construction that cannot be predicted with certainty. They write, "What the concept or 'problem' of identity forces us to acknowledge is that discovery of self through alignment with others is more a choice than a given fate, especially in the contemporary era. Furthermore, the language signifying such choice is diversified (hybrid or polyglot) rather than uniform, and it is performative (creating effects in the world) rather than just descriptive or indicative" (101). Heath's and Lareau's research helps us see how class is a powerful factor in our conceptions of our "selves"—who we are, how we talk, where we feel we belong, but class, of course, is not the only factor. Obviously, social mobility is possible for some, and the "literacy myth" is a myth precisely because some people do change their class positions. And other factors (gender, race, ethnicity, religion, and so forth) intersect as well, adding further complexity to subject formation and identity. Collins and Blot point out that, in addition, choice plays a role, even if it is a small one, in our "alignment with others," that is, in where we see ourselves belonging and the person we see ourselves becoming, but seeing how extensive the role is that choice plays is difficult. Consider the power of the myth of the "self-made man" and the widespread resistance to affirmative action. No one "chooses" the role of a "have-not." As Collins and Blot write, "Identity, while central to discourses of culture and diversity, is difficult to pin down. It hinges on, and does not resolve, troublesome polarities: between essential versus constructed tradition and group-bound versus voluntarily chosen affiliations. Such dichotomies also inform the dynamics of language, literacy, and identity . . ." (104). We operate from numerous subject positions, many of which demand a variety of discursive practices if we are to negotiate among them successfully.

Of course, we can choose not to negotiate some of them. As a first-year college student, I briefly majored in theater and imagined myself on the stage in major important roles. Eagerly I read for the part of Antigone but was mortified when the director advised me to get rid of my thick Texas accent if I wanted a shot at future roles. I had never considered my accent to be a "problem" and, truthfully, had been unaware of having an accent at all, but I immediately enrolled in a voice and articulation course and worked diligently to eradicate all traces of my working-class Texas background from my diction and speech patterns. I made a choice to try to negotiate my way more successfully among the discourses of theater professors and theater majors but, in doing so, erased aural evidence of my class and regional background and distanced myself even more from my family and old friends. Of course, I can "thicken" my accent at will, but having a choice—and, more important, being conscious that it is a choice—marks still another significant difference from those who do not have that choice to make. One change engenders another in a chain of change.

Maureen Hourigan in *Literacy as Social Exchange: Intersections of Class, Gender, and Culture* describes her work with basic writing students and illustrates the "gaps between students' desires and those of their teachers" (51). But she argues that identifying those gaps is easy compared to trying to figure out what to do about those gaps. Hourigan wants to figure out how to breach the division between her students' goals and her goals and between her students' definitions of success and her own. Determining why some students—even those in basic writing classes—experience no such gap and identify with their teachers at times more than they do with their peers, however, is also important. As a former teacher of basic writing at an open admissions university, I recall the students who came to class early to talk with me or stayed after class to talk more about their reading and writing. I taught a surprising number of students who were avid readers of science fiction or romance novels or mysteries, students who wrote poetry and fiction, students who, despite their poor public school educations, wanted desperately to find and see themselves as intellectuals. I recall one particular student who came to show me the amazing book he had stumbled on to in the library: Mortimer Adler's *How to Read a Book*. He was elated because Adler gave him a focus and a plan for his voracious, formerly random reading. These were not students who had been misplaced into basic writing; they had not done well on placement tests, and they struggled with the reading and writing required in their classes. But they were also not anything like the stereotypical basic writing students who made my colleagues question the school's open admissions policy. Instead, these were students who, defying predictions to the contrary, wanted what we were teaching.

What do we make, then, of those of us who identified more with our teachers—or if not our teachers, then the lives we found in books—than with our own families or friends? Is this desire teachable? Collins and Blot write, "Discomfort with self, who we are and where we come from, may be a common human predicament, but that should not blind us to variation in the severity and consequences of this self-estrangement, nor to the historical specificities contributed by one's class, gender, and race to the tribulations of the self" (119). In other words, to some extent we all experience periods of alienation, of not feeling at home in our own skin, but "historical specificities" affect us all differently. Dalton Conley's research in his book *Pecking Order: Which Siblings Succeed and Why,* for instance, focuses on differences among siblings. We would expect that siblings in the same family would be more similar than different in terms of class, tastes, and the like. But Conley reveals that siblings commonly have radically different responses to the same set of circumstances with radically different results. My husband has three sisters. Of the four of them, he and one sister have gone on for postbaccalaureate degrees; another sister has taken courses and completed certification programs in community colleges; the fourth sister completed high school only. Their parents both have bachelor's degrees or higher. My husband is an artist with an M.F.A.; one sister is a CPA (who majored in English); another works in computer-assisted design in the oil exploration industry; the fourth is currently a stay-at-home mother and housewife. Further complicating the picture is that two of the sisters are identical twins. I joke that if they did not resemble each other physically, I would never know that they were related. They grew up in the same house to college-educated parents yet have widely varying interests and abilities and differ socioeconomically as well, with one having moved from middle class to working class. As Collins and Blot put it, "Identities are built, constructed, with the discursive resources which are our birthright, our 'mother tongues,' but also with other, competing discourses of street, school, and workplace" (119). Some of us identify with our parents, some of us identify more strongly with our peers, and some of us, for whatever reasons, identify with a way of life foreign to our families and friends—perhaps typically described as a desire for "something more."

Such desire is not predictable. As I mentioned at the beginning of this chapter, my colleague described her desire for "something more" as born from her sense of alienation from her family and socioeconomic circumstances. Individuals who work to leave their working-class backgrounds commonly experience alienation or a sense of not fitting in with family and peers, according to Alfred Lubrano in his book *Limbo: Blue Collar Roots, White Collar Dreams.* Lubrano, a reporter for the *Philadelphia Enquirer,* interviewed more than 100 people born to working-class parents who moved into the middle class. Lubrano calls these people "Straddlers." He writes, "They are the first in their families to have graduated from college. As such they straddle two worlds, many of them not feeling at home in either, living in a kind of American limbo" (2). Similar to Heath's findings, Lubrano's research indicates that class, in a very real and felt sense, supercedes factors of race and ethnicity as his interviewees "tell strikingly similar tales of the seldom-heard, dark side of mobility" (2). Although he uses education as his class marker, he is also careful to say that education is only one factor out of many. Yet education works well for my project as I use his research to see how people describe their transition from one class to another.

Lubrano employs the modernist definition of a unified self as he argues that "[b]y ignoring class distinctions, people may be overlooking important parts of themselves and failing to understand who they really are" (5). Yet he is careful not to claim class as some sort of concrete, essential signifier. Rather, he describes class as "a metaphor that marks your place in the world. It's invisible and inexact, but it has resonance and deep meaning" (5). Class colors us and shapes us in ways that we may not be aware of but that have significant and, at times, unexpected effect. Several years ago, I took my daughter on college visits, a process so common that it was a subplot for an episode of *The Sopranos*. I loved traveling with my daughter, having that time alone with her, and I certainly loved telling others that I was taking her to colleges I only could have dreamed of (had I even known of their existence) at her age. But I hated the visits themselves. Only in writing this book was I able to begin to understand what drove me into such a state of anxiety that I paid extra for us to fly home a day early. I felt utterly out of place and intimidated; making small talk with the other parents and the administrators of these small liberal arts college was painful. I was even intimidated by the self-assured sophomore who led the tour on one campus.

Of course, that is not to say I would have been more comfortable in a more characteristically working-class environment. Describing his own relationship to his working-class background, Lubrano writes, "My interests had always lain elsewhere. Like a lot of Straddlers, I felt dissatisfied with the neighborhood status quo. That sense of being out of step with the very people you're supposed to be like is the limbo person's first inkling that he or she is bound for other places" (12). For many of us, books are what first mark us as "odd," and increasingly books are where we turn for solace. Lubrano writes, "Straddlers remember how complicated life in the old neighborhood could get after they realized they weren't really part of the crowd. Their inability to fully fit in made them uncomfortable and rendered them quasi-outcasts" (13). I do not want to imply that all middle-class children of middle-class parents experience happy, seamlessly well-adjusted lives—although Lubrano tends to idealize middle-class life: "Middle-class kids are groomed for another life" (55). He paraphrases Patrick Finn who argues that middle-class students appreciate "why reading *Macbeth* in high school could be important years down the road" (55). Most teachers will roll their eyes at this statement, knowing that having college-educated parents is no guarantee that these "kids" will appreciate that *Macbeth*, or any other work of literature, will be of value. Of course, multiple exceptions can be found to these generalizations; to speak of "the working class" or "the middle class" will always be problematic. Yet the generalizations serve as enabling fictions that allow us to make larger points about class differences and mobility.

Lubrano helps us conceptualize another problem, that is, how to describe one's move from the working class to the middle class without demonizing or denigrating the working class. When I tell a middle-class colleague a story from my childhood, I worry that she will see it as sad or, even worse, exotic. How do we describe our experiences of prejudice, racism, sexism, anti-intellectualism, the boredom of hourly wage labor, and so forth without sounding as if we are condemning all working-class people, painting them all with the same damning brush? Of course, these experiences are not confined to individuals from the working class; prejudice is not confined to the working class. Yet, as one of Lubrano's interviewees says, "you wouldn't be class-mobile and ready to hop the first bus into White-Collar World if you were all that happy with your original circumstances" (27). I am extremely proud of some elements of my background, including my work ethic and my appreciation and awareness of the work others do for me. (I am always shocked when colleagues do not speak to or know the names of the custodians for our building, for instance.) But I also celebrate my middle-class status and continue to be astonished that I have a doctorate, tenure, and a reliable income. As an old friend says in praise of our academic careers, "Inside work. No heavy lifting." Our careers are, indeed, something to be celebrated for those of us who could so easily have lived our lives under radically—and physically—different circumstances.

Of course, teachers from the middle class can understand the desire to "rise" above one's beginnings, but beginning to understand the costs and the tensions that such a rise can produce is also important. Lubrano explains:

> Of course, for many of us, the goal *is* the middle class—specifically, a more comfortable life of less backbreaking work and greater reward than our parents knew. But we don't want to have to totally reject who we are and where we came from to become educated and live in nicer houses. There is, then, unease in the transition, because Straddlers are making a difficult journey. The trip is invisible to the middle class, who don't have to cross class lines to become educated. (82)

One of my goals in writing this book is to make the "trip" more visible so all teachers may gain some sense of what fuels their students' ambivalences in the classroom or why some may find their trips include a lot of detours along the way. To accomplish this, I turn to several working-class literacy narratives,

narratives that cross lines of gender, race, and ethnicity but, as Lubrano noted regarding his own interviews, "express remarkably similar emotions" and "tell strikingly similar tales" (2). How do these writers born to the working class describe their relationship to literacy? What role does literacy play in the transition from working class to middle class? What role do schools and teachers play in their "journey"? What lessons can teachers take from these narratives? Can teachers teach the desire for education, and would that mean that they are also teaching a desire to reject the backgrounds of their working-class students?

In *The Mind at Work: Valuing the Intelligence of the American Worker*, Mike Rose writes, " . . . there are delicate social issues here. How do you encourage young people to consider college, take the right courses, perhaps leave their peers behind, look to work other than the work their parents do—how do you do that in a way that doesn't diminish who their parents are or how they make a living?" (189). In other words, how do we balance the desire to prepare our students to be upwardly mobile with the need to respect and honor their parents' work and background? I push first-generation college students in my classroom to question and think critically, knowing from my own experience of hourly wage jobs that the very last thing my bosses wanted from me was to think critically. Yet I have to assume that those students' presence in my university classroom signifies their own desire to do something other than the kinds of labor typically defined as working class.

Furthermore, as Lubrano points out, many Straddlers recall feeling like "quasi-outcasts" and do not "fit in" among peers or family members. In *An American Story*, Debra Dickerson describes her childhood of poverty with a loving mother but controlling, abusive father and her seeking out the military to help her achieve her educational and career goals, going on to earn a JD and two political science degrees. She writes, "My love of books was tolerated in our no-nonsense household, but not encouraged" (xiv). Compare this to Schwartz's description of her family as being "people of the book." Dickerson is a misfit in her neighborhood ("When I tried to be a part of the neighborhood goings-on, I floundered") and at her school, a predominantly white school for gifted children ("[m]eanwhile, at school I was just as much on the fringes as in my own community") (38). She writes:

> It's hard to say which had more to do with my isolation—my special schooling or my self-imposed physical distance. My mother used to have to order me outside to play. She'd send me outdoors, only to knock me flat onto the back porch when she'd open the door to hang out the wash; I'd be leaning against the door reading a book, technically outside but as close as possible to the safety of the house. (38)

I would wager that Dickerson's memory of being forced outside "to play" resonates with many of us. I can even remember my mother wrestling the book

I was reading from my hands so I could not take it outside, and I distinctly recall feeling at a loss about what to do outside without that precious book. In *Scenes of Instruction: A Memoir*, Michael Awkward describes himself :

> a pouty, teary-eyed boy, unable to assume a happy-go-lucky attitude or to shake the sadness of remembered and unremembered life experiences. I was aware of constantly trying to prepare myself for the next trauma, the next disappointment, the next conflict, resigned to the inevitability of serious, all-consuming, long-lasting pain, and hoping merely for the wherewithal to survive it. (16)

Added to this difficulty is physical disfigurement; he writes, "More debilitating than being poor, and certainly more of a problem than being black, was the fact that I was permanently disfigured when I was two years old" (17). Awkward's melancholy as well as the scars from grease burns marks him as other in his family and in his neighborhood.

Novelist and former columnist Anna Quindlen, in her literacy narrative *How Reading Changed My Life*, speculates "readers are dissatisfied people, yearning to be elsewhere, to live vicariously through words in a way we cannot live directly through life. Perhaps we are the world's great nomads, if only in our minds" (70). Recalling her childhood penchant for running away, she writes, "Perhaps only a truly discontented child can become as seduced by books as I was. Perhaps restlessness is a necessary corollary of devoted literacy" (4). Quindlen's speculations seem to be supported by others—Dickerson's and Awkward's, for example—narratives of growing up as the "odd ducks" with a passion for literacy in working-class families in which no one shared or valued that passion.

The metaphor of *escape* figures prominently in these narratives as well. Quindlen offers a warmer definition of *escape* when she describes books as a "haven,": "And as it was for me when I was young and surrounded by siblings, as it is today when I am surrounded by children, reading continues to provide an escape from a crowded house into an imaginary room of one's own" (31). Reading becomes a way to carve out space for oneself, a way to get away from the constant needs of others. She further wonders if this need for "escape" that reading provides is, perhaps, more true for women than for men because women are the ones most consistently called on to anticipate and meet the needs of their husbands and children. In *Red Dirt: Growing Up Okie*, Roxanne Dunbar-Ortiz immerses herself in books to remove herself from the realities of poverty and her mother's worsening mental illness. Michael Awkward's literacy emerges from a lifelong project both to escape from and to make sense of his alcoholic mother's life and their relationship through the theoretical lens of feminist theory: "This book [*Scenes of Instruction*] constitutes my risky attempt to circulate the major themes of my mother's narratives, and to demonstrate

that I've absorbed their form and content well enough to contribute to feminism's efforts to challenge patriarchy's rule" (7). Debra Dickerson, too, reads to
escape physically and emotionally from poverty but also from a controlling and,
at times, physically abusive father. She writes, "My own life had to be muffled in
heavy cloth, but on the printed page my emotions ranged free" (68).

Alfred Lubrano calls these families "black hole families": "Black holes are
dense, dark stars whose gravitational pull is so great that no light can escape.
The universe burns with constellations of dull stars. If you're part of such a
family, you have a choice: You can succumb to parental fiat and stay true blue
collar, your light forever dim, or you can buck the folks and pay a price for
your incandescence" (34). Of course, the family "constellation" is more complex than this as Lubrano's own family and story show. He writes, "My father
held himself out as a negative object lesson. If you don't do your homework,
ace the test, and apply to college, you'll wind up laying bricks. You'll wind up
being just like me. What does that make a father feel like, to have to instruct
his son not to be like his old man?" (27). In some families, then, a complex of
factors both pushes and pulls family members together and apart. My parents
were always uncomfortable with my being "smart" and were visibly relieved
when my grades dropped in high school. I do not remember ever being told to
do homework or pull my grades up when I came home with C's or D's once
I returned to school after dropping out. Having and keeping a part-time job
was far more important than grades to my parents, yet they would be horrified
at the idea that they were "holding me back"—or, worse, pulling me into their
"black hole." More likely, they wanted me to fit in with them and the people
they knew, and money was definitely in short supply.

Lubrano rightly asks, "If children can simply educate themselves away,
where will the parent fit in their new world?" (33). Parents many times know
better than their children that education will separate them on many levels.
That separation comes at a cost paid over time in many ways. In "Writing on
the Bias," Linda Brodkey writes, for instance, of her desire for a private space
such as those described in the novels she read:

> I have no idea if many other children from working-class homes also acquired
> from their reading an appetite for privacy. But I am certain that the literature
> that fascinated me kindled and shaped a desire for privacy in me so acute
> that only hearing my mother's voice reminds me that not only I but an entire
> family paid the price of my replacing the sociality of my working-class home
> with the books that now keep me company. (538)

Anna Quindlen, who unfailingly sees the passion for literacy in a positive light,
quotes Roald Dahl's *Matilda*, perhaps the ultimate literacy story for children:
"'She [Matilda] had learned something comforting, . . . that we are not alone'"
(38). So literacy can be simultaneously isolating and comforting. As a child,

I spent time each summer in a large house shared with my widowed grand-mother and her many unmarried siblings, all of whom lived together their entire lives. Each summer they devised and chipped in on activities (such as swimming and diving lessons) for me not only because they wanted me to be entertained, but also because they were concerned about the amount of time I spent oblivious to everything but the book I was reading. Now that it is too late, of course, I wish I had spent more time with my many great aunts, all independent women with full lives. There was much to be learned there that I missed. Yet in bad times, books provided very real and much-needed solace.

Brodkey also argues that her literacy led her to be placed in college-placement classes, thereby separating her further from her working-class family. She writes, "Like reading, tracking radically displaced me, conferring on me honorary middle-class privileges . . ." (542). Being tracked into college preparatory classes, Brodkey finds herself in contact with the middle-class children of middle-class parents, invited into their middle-class homes, where she "learned to speak fluent bourgeois" (542). The difficulty can be that although we may be able to visit our middle-class friends in their homes, we may not want them to visit us in our working-class homes. When my father came home from work, especially in hot Texas summers, he would strip down to his boxer shorts as soon as possible, and I was mortified by his table manners. On the very rare occasions I had a friend over for dinner, we would either take our plates to another room or my parents and I would conduct the meal on constrained "good" behavior that left little room for pleasure. School can certainly open doors to other worlds and other ways of living in those worlds for individuals, but those doors can easily swing closed behind them and leave families behind.

A working-class child may take some time to learn that her school-learned literacy lessons may not be welcomed at home or in the neighborhood. Debra Dickerson and Victor Villanueva both describe correcting their parents' speech or usage. Dickerson writes, "I began to correct my elders; having Mama slap my face on the spot of the transgression broke me of that habit. Street fights cured me with my peers. So I kept my knowledge to myself and wondered why people wouldn't rather know. I thought I was helping them" (37). Villanueva, too, corrects at home, but is savvy enough to know not to share his knowledge on the street: "At home I would correct my folks when an English rule was broken. Yet, even as I was dogmatic and doctrinaire at home, I understood there were different rules on the block" (8). From an early age, Villanueva's understanding of diverse discursive practices is sophisticated; he writes, "Spanish and Spanglish at home. Standard English at home and in school. Black English on the block. Different rules in different places. I knew that" (8). Villanueva, Awkward, Dickerson, and others know better than their teachers, perhaps, the importance, the flexibility, and the power of language that serves to make school both attractive and threatening. School can be the place that introduces working-class students to the pleasures of language, but it can also be the place where their "otherness" is revealed and confirmed.

So these writers exhibit ambivalence in their attitudes toward school. Michael Awkward, for example, receives numerous awards at his school for his high scores on national achievement tests and in his classes. Yet his pride in his accomplishments is tainted by the knowledge that his achievements are not based on his gifts alone but rather on his gifts relative to his classmates' in a poor school in a poor neighborhood. He skipped fourth grade, but even at that young age he was aware that his promotion had more to do with the economic realities of race and poverty than with his superior intelligence:

> . . . during my first term in George Washington [Elementary School], my fourth-grade teacher, Mrs. Robinson, recognized that I already knew all of the material she was supposed to teach me that year. I'd been a good student at my previous school, McCall, but I knew that a number of my classmates there were probably more intelligent and certainly more studious than I was. I got skipped not because I'd become appreciably smarter during the summer between third and fourth grade but because I'd moved from the outskirts of a largely white, upper-middle-class school district with an excellent elementary school to an overwhelmingly black housing project and school where the resources, parental involvement, and scholastic expectations were palpably inferior. (15)

Even at an early age (at least in his representation of himself at an early age), Awkward knows the difference between a good education and a poor or indifferent education, and he knows the differences between haves and have-nots. Living in a neighborhood with a significant Latino population, I was always placed in honors classes until my family moved to a middle-class neighborhood in my sophomore year of high school where I found myself no longer to be considered honors material. It took me much longer than it did Awkward to realize that racism against my Latino classmates most certainly contributed to my placement in honors courses and to their placement in "regular" or vocational tracks in one neighborhood. Similarly, classism most likely figured in my "demotion" from honors to "regular" classes in the "better" school and neighborhood. In addition, I experienced the reverse of Awkward's move from a good school to a poor one, as I found my old schools had not covered material I was expected to know at the new one. In my own case, however, it did not occur to me to doubt the decisions made on my behalf or to consider the possibility of inequity. I just accepted it.

Despite winning numerous academic awards, certificates, and medals, Awkward's ambivalence deepens as he begins to see how empty the recognition is in the big picture. Why is it, he wonders, that he can so obviously excel but not merit any sign of his being acknowledged and appreciated by his teachers and peers? How is doing so well yet being so ignored possible? He writes:

> . . . I felt overwhelmed, stunned, and, for reasons I couldn't quite put my finger on, bitter. If I was indeed, as the surprising results of the tests suggested, an intellectual fish, albeit in a relatively small and polluted pond, why hadn't it seemed that my teachers had taken a special interest in me or gone out of their way to nurture my talents? Why was I not a teacher's pet, not singled out, as other members of my class had been? (65)

Awkward here offers an important observation about schools. School would be the obvious place where intelligence is most overtly rewarded and appreciated, yet, as Awkward's narrative as well as others' narratives attest, schools reflect their culture. Heath's research shows us that schools reward middle-class ways of knowing and being, that is, ways of communicating, behaving, dressing, and so on. Intelligence can only go so far to overcome difference from these "norms," or, rather, those ways of knowing and being that are perceived norms. I am reminded of a conversation I had several years ago with the then-principal of the intermediate school in our small town with regard to providing more activities of an intellectual rather than an athletic nature for students—especially for gifted students—in the public schools. He stated clearly that he was interested in serving average children because the "smart kids" will take care of themselves. He certainly cared about test scores, but he saw "smart kids" as students who came to the school already smart; he did not see the school playing much of a role in making them smart or keeping them that way.

Debra Dickerson, too, finds her relationship to school conflicted and ambivalent. Her first experience of school is entirely positive. She writes, "By first grade, I was the designated 'brainiac' and good girl. I loved school, I loved teachers, and I loved books. If I didn't exactly love rules, I did accept them as a fact of life and focused on mastering, rather than resisting them" (32). However, eventually, she comes to realize, like Awkward, that the education she is receiving at her school is second-rate: "The classes had long since ceased to be challenging; the teachers resented me because I corrected them and asked questions they couldn't answer; the other kids hated me. I was such a nebbish, even my own siblings had taken to disowning me" (34). While her self-representation is less than flattering, she reveals herself to be a child desperate for knowledge and desperate to be taught—the kind of child most teachers claim they want to see in their classrooms. Dickerson's only hope is what she calls "gifted school," a predominantly white school across town to which she would have to be bused. She writes:

> I wanted that special knowledge to which only whites had access. I knew that if I stayed at Benton [her current school], stayed in my neighborhood,

I'd only know what whites wanted me to know. If I went to their school, I'd know what they knew. This was not a political act. I wasn't concerned that black people in general gain access to this special knowledge. I didn't intend to work for revolution or to help my people or cure cancer. I just wanted more. (34)

While Dickerson much later in life changes her position to be more connected to and involved in political issues, at this point, like Awkward, she is aware that more is available to middle-class whites than is available to her in her poor neighborhood, and, like Awkward, she resents that it is not available to her. Her parents, interestingly, resist her desire to attend "gifted school." Her father does not want her to go to school with whites, her mother does not want her to be bused, and both are most likely aware that education will take her away from them. A deeply religious former Marine, her father in particular holds limited ideas of what awaits her as an adult; he imagines no better than clerical or waitressing work for her.

Still she manages to convince her parents to allow her to attend the new school, but once at that new school, Dickerson is ambivalent once more: "Gifted school was wonderful. Gifted school was awful" (32). On the one hand, she acknowledges that the education she received there was far superior to any she has received since—including at Harvard Law School, and she finds there knowledgeable teachers eager to teach her. But she also learns what it is to be "a practical rather than just a statistical minority" (34). She writes, "I learned many things at Wade [the gifted school]. The first was that I was poor. The second, that I was low class" (36). Dickerson's experience tells a larger story of education in the late 1960s and early 1970s for many students of color: "We blacks in the gifted program were like Cinderella at the ball; the party was over when our special bus arrived to whisk us back to the ghetto. Our inclusion in the mainstream only lasted the duration of the school day and within the confines of the school building" (38). Her experience of education is steeped in lessons of racism and classism.

So, too, is Villanueva's, but in even more complicated ways. He describes, for instance, a lifelong ambivalence about affirmative action. Writing of himself in the third person, further emphasizing his problematic relationship to the program, Villanueva writes:

He had seen that tokenism, even when well-motivated, even though somehow necessary, makes things seem equitable when they aren't equitable at all, so that the same handful rises quickly to positions of prominence. He sees sense in Affirmative Action. He is sometimes grateful. He is often leery. He's the only portorican rhetorician he knows. In terms of others of color, the action isn't affirmative enough. In terms of his being acted on affirmatively, he always wonders if, maybe, he isn't as smart as people say he is. (13)

Although Dickerson at times may feel like an outsider, she never doubts her ability to rise to any challenge, even when, or perhaps especially when, others express their doubts. Villanueva, however, is sensitive to the dilemma affirmative action poses in our culture where we still want to believe that we can indeed raise ourselves up by our own "bootstraps" and it is our own fault if we do not do so. We ignore the special privileges accorded the middle-class that lend to middle class successes in school and beyond but are not surprised when a Victor Villanueva ponders whether he is "as smart as people say he is." But what does it say about our own educational system that Villanueva can write those words, that those words resonate, that he could leave school questioning his achievement? Of course, the progress and process of his education took circuitous routes (as did Dickerson's) by way of the military, a general education diploma (GED), and a loan-heavy, poverty-ridden trek through graduate school. Villanueva raises questions about that process and about literacy education in particular for all who find themselves wondering if they deserve to be where they are when others among their families and friends remain "behind."

Linda Brodkey also reflects on her literacy acquisition and asks startling questions that do not shed a flattering light on the teaching of writing. She writes:

> . . . when I look back I see only a young girl intent on getting it right, eager to produce flawless prose, and not a trace of the woman who years later would write that school writing is to writing as catsup to tomatoes: as junk food to food. What is nutritious has been eliminated (or nearly so) in processing. What remains is not just empty but poisonous fare because some people so crave junk that they prefer it to food, and their preference is then used by those who, since they profit by selling us catsup as a vegetable and rules as writing, lobby to keep both on the school menu. (528)

Brodkey makes serious charges here. She describes herself as a child who thrived on rules and control. Her physical metaphor for this control is her devotion to ballet that lasted through her entire childhood and adolescence and that she practiced "with all the fervor of an S & M enthusiast for I can recall making no distinctions between pleasure and pain" (531). In school, "flawless prose" equates to largely error-free prose, but prose that is more concerned with correctness than content offers little by way of nourishment; like a fast food meal deal, it fulfills the requirement (that is, it fills the stomach) but dulls the palate and, if eaten to the exclusion of "real" food, is ultimately "poisonous." Brodkey does not stop there. She goes on to charge those who "profit" from a rigid regime of rule-based writing as being as morally corrupt as those who would profit from catsup being categorized and served as a vegetable to growing children who need real nourishment. These

are harsh charges against our schools, yet as I see the effects of state-mandated testing on the students arriving at my public university, I am inclined
to agree with her.

   Those students who perform well in school tend to be those who can
function well in—or at least tolerate—the school's rule-based culture. For
many working-class students (as well as for many middle-class students) the
rules seem pointless, stupid—as admittedly many of the rules are. But Brodkey thrives in this rule-based culture where "I learned to trade my words for
grades and degrees, in what might be seen as the academic equivalent of deal-
ing in futures . . ." (529). Writing, then, is a commodity, and soon reading is,
too, and this commodification of something she has loved becomes emblematic of a "loss of innocence" when the librarians at her public library declare it
to be time for her to move up to the adult section in the library. For many, this
is a triumphant moment (as it was for me, but, then, I had to argue for the
privilege to leave the children's section), a heady moment when, what seems
like acres of cold rigidly organized shelves of books compared to the intimate
atmosphere of the children's section become available. But Brodkey sees it as
a move away from a time when reading meant stories that could be read just
to be loved to a time when reading meant literature to gain knowledge and
improve oneself, that is, great literature. Now she can no longer love reading
indiscriminately; she has to discern the "good" stories from the less worthy
ones. Reading for entertainment is no longer the first priority.

   The metaphor of commodification serves to describe this transition as
well. She appropriated the stories in the children's library as her stories without thought of provenance or ownership. Brodkey writes, "In the child's economics of literacy, the cycle of exchange depended entirely on *her* reading"
(532). Brodkey argues that this view is "dangerous" because it is blind to the
material reality of book production, but she points out that this is a result of
schools' and libraries' exalting reading and ignoring writing, especially in the
early grades. In the adult section of the library, however, she becomes aware
that "every book belonged to an author" and is, therefore, not her property
(532). In addition, she comes to see these books ranked and some are deemed
more valuable than others. Brodkey writes, "The economics of literature is
entirely different from that of stories." She then points out:

> the value of stories as measured against literature is very low indeed. Stories
> are a dime a dozen. Literature is scarce. Almost anyone can tell or write sto-
> ries (even a child can do it). Not just anyone can write literature (most adults
> cannot), and not just anyone can read it. Literature is an acquired taste, it
> seems, and like a taste for caviar and martinis, it is acquired through associat-
> ing with the right people, whose discernment guarantees a steady demand for
> a limited supply of literature. (533–34)

So everyone can consume and produce stories; stories are the product of a democratic literacy available to all, but because this literacy is available to all, its value is lower. The move from stories to literature winnows out many readers, and for many, if not most, that winnowing takes place in school where we are trained to value literature as well as rules. If we do not value either, we tend to blame that failure on ourselves. But literature and rules are hardly equally valued. One is read, the other is written—or, rather, to recall Brodkey's metaphor of junk food, literature is haute cuisine to be savored, whereas writing is a Happy Meal to be swallowed and forgotten. Brodkey writes, "Only when I began studying and teaching writing did I finally remember that esthetics can be as effective a hermetic seal against the economic and political conditions of authorship as are industrial parks and affluent suburbs against the economic privation and desperation of the urban and rural poor" (534). Literature continues, then, to function as a class marker, and school writing, the writing done in our schools, to satisfy teachers who also teach literature, is to writing "as junk food [is] to food" (528).

Brodkey goes on to further condemn how writing has been and continues to be conceived, taught, and reproduced in the typical classroom:

> Over the years, the schools have probably quelled a desire to write in a good many children by subjecting them to ritual performances of penmanship, spelling, grammar, punctuation, organization, and most recently thinking. Every generation mixes its own nostrums and passes them off as writing. The fetishes may change but not the substitution of some ritual performance for writing. (531)

If we think of each of these "ritual performances" as a hurdle to jump before we are allowed to move to "real" writing, I am amazed that any of us ever choose to commit another word to a page. For several years, I judged a regional level of a statewide academic competition called "Ready Writing." Contestants competed by writing on a surprise topic, and the three strongest received awards and were then able to compete at the next level. I was astonished to see students quoting in their essays when they had no prior knowledge of what the prompt was to be. I learned that teachers were instructing their students to memorize several "all-purpose" quotations by famous people to insert somewhere (usually the introduction or conclusion) in their essays. These students were being taught to prepare their essays as much as possible to produce grammatically correct, clearly organized essays that all sounded alarmingly alike even though the students came from different schools in different school districts. What I saw consistently in the three or four years that I organized and judged the competition, however, was that the best writers showed evidence of engagement with the topic and of a long immersion in language—and did not make use of *Bartlett's Familiar Quotations*. Generally, the contestants from the most affluent high school in our region, a highly competitive school with a huge tax base and a vast majority of college-educated parents and college-bound students, won with ease. But we would almost always have one winner from a rural, poor school, a winner who like Brodkey, Awkward, and Dickerson, loved books, loved reading, and felt an intense desire to write.

Certainly, at times our schools seem actively to seek to extinguish their students' desire to read and write. My daughter began sixth grade eager to start the term, bored with hanging around the house. How did her school greet her eagerness? Administrators and teachers took turns reading the many-page student handbook aloud to an auditorium full of fifth and sixth graders, then made them take a multiple-choice test over what they had heard. It took two days. If any students had entered the building eager to get started, the school made sure they did not exit that way. Fortunately my daughter and students in general are resilient and many learn despite their schools' (or parents') blunders. Later in the same school system, a teacher encouraged my daughter to write like Jack Kerouac after she had been swept away by his hipster prose. She worked hard for that teacher, and he responded with praise but also with respect for her as an intellectual. Individual teachers have significant effect every day, even in the most repressive circumstances.

Furthermore, literacy narratives reveal that a desire to read and write is not as easily extinguished as we might imagine. Anna Quindlen argues that pleasure reading (not the reading of "great" literature) can lead to writing. "For some of us, reading begets rereading, and rereading begets writing" (52). She argues, "In fact one of the most pernicious phenomena in assigned reading is the force-feeding of serious work at an age when the reader will feel pushed away, not from the particular book being assigned, but from an entire class of books, or even books in general" (55). Quindlen maintains that what made her want to write was reading books such as Booth Tarkington's popular book for girls *Seventeen*. She also recalls observing her parents enjoying "lightweight" humorous and romantic reading. Even in my "book-poor" house, I remember seeing my father absorbed with *Inside Detective* and chuckling over the "Humor in Uniform" section of *Reader's Digest*. Texts such as these convinced Quindlen that producing these sorts of reading for others was something that she, too, could do. She asks, "And if readers use words and stories as much, or more, to lessen human isolation as to expand human knowledge, is that somehow unworthy, invalid, and unimportant"? (38). I would substitute the word *writing* for *reading* and ask the same question of our schools.

How much of the writing done in school strikes students as empty, meaningless, exercises? When I taught basic writing several years ago, I worked to help my students pass the state-mandated writing test. One semester, two came back from the test dejected. Their writing prompt required that they argue for or against community recycling; outraged, they pointed out to me that in their inner-city neighborhoods, recycling was not an option, and they were grateful just to have the garbage regularly collected at all. Yes, more skillful writers and students more thoroughly immersed in literacy would have been able to grind out five paragraphs taking one side or the other without having to do much thinking, but on a very real level, I share their outrage. The prompt writers not only obviously did not engage these students, but they also blatantly excluded them or, worse yet, could not even allow for their existence. Imagining this writing begetting other writing is difficult. Neither student passed, leaving both more convinced that their goal of a college education is that much less attainable and that, at least to a degree, their failure is not merely accidental or the result of their own deficiencies.

Michael Awkward makes little mention of writing in school although naturally we assume he did. His substantive discussion of writing occurs at the very beginning of his book where he attempts to justify his project and his identification as a black male feminist. He also addresses the difficulty of acknowledging our individual lives and the roles they play in our scholarship; scholarly writing attempts to erase the personal. The limitations inherent in academic writing lead him to the personal narrative. He writes, "Certainly, my own training limits my capacity, when I am performing traditional scholarly tasks, to deal cogently with the idiosyncrasies of my intellectual journey. But because speaking of that journey remains important to me, I have turned . . . to autobiographical writing" (3). His concern that identity politics have served master narratives about what being working class, African American, or physically challenged means compel him to produce his particular narrative of a particular life: " . . . formulations of group identity can be used to predict or help account for individual behaviors and attitudes. But we are also all aware that individuals maintain some degree of power to determine how they respond to external stimuli. None of us is doomed to perform others' elaborate scripts of race, gender, or other social circumstances" (3). In other words, we can make general predictions about the commonalities of experience most likely to be shared among members of certain groups, as in Alfred Lubrano's use of the term *limbo* to refer to how those who make the shift from working class to middle class never feel exactly "at home" in either class and his referring to those who experience "limbo" as "Straddlers." But Awkward states that individuals will experience those commonalities differently. In Awkward's case, he describes his lifelong efforts to understand what his mother's admonitions not to be like their abusive, negligent father mean for him and his family, and those efforts can be seen as, in a real sense, leading him to his academic life as a feminist scholar of African-American literature. He writes that his "book constitutes my risky attempt to circulate the major themes of my mother's narratives, and to demonstrate that I've absorbed their form and content well enough to contribute to feminism's efforts to challenge patriarchy's unabated rule" (7). Awkward's mother's story is intertwined with his own, and both are intertwined with his life's work and his writing.

Debra Dickerson, too, makes no mention of school writing. Once she moves from the gifted school, she finds that because her neighborhood school is so weak, she has to take responsibility for her own education by "reading, reading, reading": "I carried a heavy backpack everywhere for fear I'd finish one book . . . and not have another at the ready" (68). But regarding writing, she states, " . . . I was twenty years away from even attempting to fill a page; if people like me couldn't be lawyers [as her father had asserted], they certainly could not write" (68). Not until twenty years later, after a successful career in the U.S. Air Force and during her first year of Harvard Law School, does she begin to write in earnest and with pleasure: "To this day, I have no idea why or how I started writing. I'd always done it effortlessly but never saw any future in it, if only because writers were gods to me. . . . I suppose it was finally having the luxury of entertaining thoughts . . . directly aimed at survival" (252–53). Dickerson claims to have no clear sense of what motivates her to write, but near the end of her book, she offers an anecdote of her response to a white male friend's description of her as "elite." At first she is incensed as she recalls the toll moving from poor working class to the middle class has taken, the class markers that she has discarded and acquired along the way. But then she realizes in both practical and material terms that she has indeed become "elite." She writes:

> No world traveler with a B.A., M.A., and Ivy League J.D. can pretend to be one of the proletariat, no matter her origins. I can understand it. I can commiserate with it. I can suffer, through loved ones, the very real tragedies visited upon those who think they've escaped. I can remain involved, I can fight for its rights, I can tell its stories. What I can't do is claim more than honorary membership. All I can do is stand ready to be of assistance and to take advantage of my unique vantage point. (277)

This strikes me as a powerful statement that makes a couple of important claims. For one thing, Dickerson makes clear that her class movement disqualifies her as a representative voice of the black working class—she can claim only "honorary membership" now. The same transition that distances us from our working-class family and peers prevents us from representing their positions or interests. For another thing, Dickerson clearly identifies a motive to write, that is, "to tell its stories" from her "unique vantage point."

As Quindlen, Awkward, and Dickerson show us, desire emerges from connections and possibilities—connections between the writer and the world and the possibility that the writer can have effect. Victor Villanueva uses the phrase *rising consciousness* (which he associates closely with "critical consciousness").

Returning from military service in Korea, he is struck by his realization that the tactics of then-President Pak's repressive "democratic" regime and the resistance to his oppressive rule receive virtually no attention in the United States—even though U.S. soldiers are stationed there and see the effects of his abuses of power. Villanueva offers this as a small epiphany. Referring to himself in third person, he writes, "He begins to wonder how such big events could be so effectively kept from so many" (64). As a student in community college, where "[w]riting is 200 words on anything, preceded by a sentence outline" (67), Villanueva is it flattered when a teacher suspects him of plagiarizing; it means he can write.

In graduate school, writing becomes the appropriation of each professor's style, reproduced after close reading of his or her publications in the library, so that along with rising consciousness comes an even deeper awareness of differences in discursive practices, building on his earlier awareness that Standard English, Spanglish, and street talk all have their places and uses. Dreadfully poor, he pushes on with graduate school, largely "because he thinks he can, despite all that had said he could not" (71), calling himself the "outsider obsessed" (73). His drive for higher literacy is certainly seated in deep desire and an ongoing attention to the ways people are kept from knowing—kept from knowing of repression in Korea, kept from knowing what constitutes "correct" form in a graduate literature class, kept from college preparatory classes. Villanueva returns to the concept of "critical consciousness" in his conclusion: "We need to cling to our various collectivities—Puerto Rican, Latino, of color, academic, American—and they need not be mutually exclusive if we consider them critically, and if we accept that we carry contradictions. We all stand to gain by developing critical consciousness" (143). Villanueva's critical consciousness led him to write a narrative attempting to make sense of his own academic journey. Can we then argue that a desire to write can arise from rising critical consciousness?

Quindlen, Awkward, Dickerson, and Villanueva all offer us ways to understand the motivation to write and all can be seen to have found themselves, in Brodkey's terms, "writing on the bias." Brodkey's extended metaphor originates in her memories of her mother's sewing as she realizes, "I must have learned to write from watching my mother sew" (544). When sewing, one lays out pattern pieces across the fabric at an angle rather than with the weave running up and down, parallel and perpendicular to the pattern, so that the garment, when finished, will hang evenly. Brodkey writes, "A bias may be provided by a theory or an experience or an image or an ideology. Without a bias, however, language is only words as cloth is only threads" (546). In other words, we begin by having something to say and a position from which to say it. She continues, "To write is to find words that explain what can be seen from an angle of vision, the limitations of which determine a wide or narrow bias, but not the lack of one" (546). Instead of encouraging students to find and write from a bias, however, Brodkey argues that schools work to prevent it with rules that forbid the use of first person, for instance, and that a result can be eradication of the writer's authority. Writing becomes rules rather than ideas, ideas that mean something to the writer. Of course, adherence to rules is easy to measure—as is the failure to adhere. Writing as meaningful exploration is only "incidental" to the curriculum; those who grow up loving to write tend not to have acquired that love in school, and many report the opposite to be true.

Brodkey's critique is aimed at more than just public schools and includes college composition courses because they are similarly taught in many institutions across the country as well. She writes:

> That this country has historically substituted tokens of literacy for literacy practices and then cloaked its anti-intellectualism in alarming statistics about illiteracy and illiterates makes it all the more important that those of us who have learned to write teach ourselves to remember how and where that happened, what it was we learned, and especially how the lessons learned from an unofficial curriculum protected us from the proscriptions that have ruthlessly dominated the official curriculum from the outset. (547)

What does it indicate in the literacy narratives discussed herein that none of the writers offers loving memories of being taught to write in school? What does it indicate when school itself is in many instances described in painful terms?

Quindlen, Awkward, Dickerson, and Villanueva all offer "lessons learned from the unofficial curriculum." Quindlen decides she can be a writer from observing her own and her family's responses to popular—not "great"—fiction. Awkward is moved to write, in part at least, by his need to make sense of his relationship to his abused, alcoholic mother. Dickerson only begins to love to write when that writing has no connection to academia but instead helps her connect to and make peace with her place in the world. Villanueva writes to make a place for himself as well—a place for the "portorican rhetorician"—and all that implies. As Brodkey concludes, "Writing is seated in desires as complicated as those that give rise to dancing and sewing, where the rules of play are also subject to the contingencies of performance" (547). Writing that matters emerges from desire, but desire rarely emerges from rules. The question remains, however, whether students can be taught desire and whether schools can find ways to tap the desire already there.

One factor that brings Quindlen, Awkward, Dickerson, Villanueva, and Brodkey's projects together is their desire to own their stories by crafting them and telling them to others. Like Bruner, Patrick Shannon argues that "[s]tories are how people make sense of themselves and their worlds" (xi) and that ownership is a key to literacy acquisition. In *Text, Lies, and Videotape: Stories about Life, Literacy, and Learning*, Shannon writes:

> In young children's spontaneous stories that they act out as they play, we can see how they believe people relate to one another, who they hope to become, and how they will behave. We can see adolescents play roles in their own and other people's stories in order to figure out where they fit into their ever-expanding worlds. As adults, the true and imaginary stories we wish to tell and believe suggest what we value most in this world. In a real sense, stories make people. (xi)

At every stage of our lives, stories are working on us, and we, in turn, are working on them, trying on different ways of being in the world and different ways of understanding the world around us. This is one of the many reasons I love working with first-year students; so many of them, traditional as well as nontraditional, are trying on new personas, taking the beginning of college as another chance to negotiate and explore their identities, testing waters and testing ideas.

Negotiation is another key factor for Shannon's view of literacy acquisition. He argues, "[W]e read and write our lives as if they were texts and we negotiate meaning from and with those texts. Negotiation is necessary because meaning is neither exclusively in the text nor in our heads" (xii). Of course, we are bombarded with texts, and we have to make our ways through and with those texts each day. This negotiation among many texts, the ability to put them together and make meaning, is what shows us to be literate, and the better we are able to negotiate many and varied texts, the more literate we are. As Shannon writes:

> My ability to use those negotiated meanings in order to make sense of my life, history, and culture; to make connections between my life and those of others; and to take action upon what I learn about myself and the world gives me some power and enables me to have some control over my life. This literacy empowers me to read and write the past, the present, and the future—it offers me the freedom to explore and act. (xii–xiii)

Shannon sees a clear conjunction between literacy and power, and, given this conjunction, what can be more empowering for those from marginalized backgrounds than to produce a life narrative that inevitably becomes a literacy narrative? These writers, in publishing their narratives, demonstrate their "ability to use those negotiated meanings in order to make sense of [their] life, history, and culture." In a very real sense, they own their stories.

Ownership, however is not a simple relationship between owner and owned. Shannon argues that a reductive definition of ownership leads us to see in limited and individualistic terms. We love to see ourselves as singular, unique individuals, influenced only by our singular, unique tastes and opinions. My students, for instance, frequently argue that they are immune to advertising's allure; they buy Nike or Adidas or another brand name because of their singular, unique taste—not because advertisements or their peers influenced them. Convincing them otherwise is not easy because they (and, of course, the advertising industry as well) have a lot invested in seeing themselves (that is, in reading their personal texts) in that light. But Shannon points out, "If people are to come to understand themselves and others through literacy, then they must push past the illusion of singular personal ownership and voice to acknowledge the social groups who speak thorough them. In this way, we can locate ourselves in the social constellations that surround us" (31). So, for Shannon, comprehending and acknowledging something of how and where we are positioned is important, as is positioning ourselves among the social groups (and I would add discourse communities) in which we circulate.

But the work does not stop here. We still have to question our relationships to our race, class, ethnicity, gender, and social groups to interrogate how we do and do not fit in, how these groups do or do not describe or include us, what we take and reject from these groups, and so on. Shannon writes:

> Once the multiple ownership is identified, we can examine, argue with, and decide what it is that we hope to stand for and what it is that we once were but which we no longer want to be. Only after we explore the multiple ownership of our words and deeds can we develop intellectual autonomy through sorting out contradicting values, attitudes, and beliefs within them. (35)

As Brodkey might say we scrutinize the cloth to find the bias. Debra Dickerson's *An American Story* is a perfect case in point. As a child and adolescent, she identifies herself as a "Poindexter," alienated from peers and, at times, family members. As a young adult serving in the U.S. Air Force, she defines herself as a Reagan Republican, believing that people deserve what they get and acknowledging no significant connection between herself and other African Americans. Only in her mid-thirties does she begin to interrogate her characterization of herself and of the multiple groups she belongs to and, thereby, to understand that she cannot cut herself off from those groups; those groups produced her. Dickerson writes, "I hadn't understood then that you can never stop being who you were born being; you can add things but you can never subtract from the baseline" (276). In acknowledging herself as a person who can accurately be described as "elite" but also has the "special vantage point" of growing up in a poor working-class family, she also begins to come to terms with where she comes from and how she got where she is. That need to examine multiple ownership surely makes the journey from there to here—the narrative itself—possible.

But the question remains, how do we bring desire and ownership into the classroom at a time when, as Christopher Schroeder argues, "even for the prototypical white, middle-class student, the cultural capital of the academy can be, and increasingly is, foreign and other" (10)? And what does it mean that, based on my reading of many working-class literacy narratives and my own experience, we find a seemingly shared sense of "alienation," as the anecdotal opening of this chapter suggests, from our own working-class families and peers? What does it mean that the best indicator of a working-class student's likelihood of academic success may be his or her dissatisfaction with his or her working-class lives or families or both? Do "dissatisfied people" make the best readers, as Anna Quindlen suggests? What seems to be indicated in the reading of these working-class narratives is that, for some, the desire for higher literacy cannot be "quelled" and drives us in ways that, in many cases, make no sense to our working-class families and peers. Victor Villanueva and his family lived on food stamps while he worked on his graduate degrees and worked as a teaching assistant. The colleague I referred to at the beginning of this chapter had her parents send her cases of tuna as Christmas presents each year to help her survive on her teaching assistantship stipend. How many of us flirted with bankruptcy as we paid for trips to the MLA conferences incurring credit card debt we could not afford? Is a willingness to live, many of us with families, under this kind of deprivation necessarily a good thing? And should we expect our students to approach this level of desire that, when viewed from outside academia, does not appear entirely rational?

Granted, these narratives comprise a limited sample that does not offer much hope to those of us who want to believe that we have the potential to make all students, regardless of their backgrounds or their family lives, passionate about acquiring higher literacy. The following and final chapter will examine alternate sites of literacy pedagogy, sites away from the classroom, to see what they, too, may offer teachers of composition.

Chapter Six

Reading with Pleasure

What Oprah Can Teach Us about Literacy Sponsorship

In his essay collection *How to Be Alone*, Jonathan Franzen considers the state of contemporary literacy and his own life as a reader and writer of novels. In "Why Bother?" he explores the decline in an audience for "serious" or "substantive" fiction, the kind of fiction he writes. Franzen characterizes his concern, and subsequent depression, about the decline of "serious" readers as "despair about the American novel" (55). His reading of a novel, Paula Fox's novel *Desperate Characters*, "saved him as a reader" but he still found himself "succumbing, as a novelist, to despair about the possibility of connecting the personal and the social" (58). His desire is to be a writer of fiction that matters, that makes a difference in people's lives and makes a difference in the culture, yet he acknowledges sadly the "failure of my culturally engaged novel to engage with the culture. I'd intended to provoke; what I got was sixty reviews in a vacuum" (61). "The dollar," he opines, "is now the yardstick of cultural authority" (62).

Although Franzen himself critiques his concerns at the same time he displays them, his "despair" over the state and fate of reading in American culture may not be entirely misplaced. Andrew Solomon's "The Closing of the American Book," an editorial in the July 10, 2004, *New York Times*, echoes Franzen's fears in its response to a National Endowment for the Arts survey on reading habits of Americans. The survey reveals that "reading for pleasure is way down in America in every group—old and young, wealthy and poor, educated and uneducated, men and women, Hispanic, black and white."

Blaming anti-intellectualism as well as "flawed intellectualism" in the forms of poststructuralism, deconstruction, and the questioning of the Western canon, Andrew Solomon argues, "We need to teach people not only how, but also why to read. The struggle is not to make people read more, but to make them want to read more" (2). He continues, "We must weave reading back into the very fabric of the culture and make it a mainstay of community" (2).

Academic David Bleich in "What Literature Is 'Ours'?" joins the chorus bewailing the current state of the literate practices of the college students he teaches at one of the country's first-tier research institutions and expressing his concern over his students' indifference to literature and its allure. "Few students see literature as mattering; there's no 'our literature'" (288). Like Franzen, he is alarmed that students have no sense of literature playing a part in their own lives or in the life of our culture. He sees the problem not so much as a failure on readers' parts but as their having "no role" in, or no felt connection to, literature's creation, and he argues that teachers must teach "how much learning matters" (312).

In his efforts to understand reading and why some of us love it—even crave it—whereas others do not, Franzen turns to Shirley Brice Heath whose research led her to study "'enforced transition zones'—places where people are held captive without recourse to television or other comforting pursuits" to observe people's reading habits. "Whenever she saw people reading or buying 'substantive works of fiction' (meaning, roughly, trade-paperback fiction), she asked for a few minutes of their time. She visited summer writers' conferences and creative-writing programs to grill ephebes. She interviewed novelists" (75). One resulting observation of Heath's research will surprise no one: "the habit of reading works of substance must have been 'heavily modeled' when [the reader] was very young" (75). Of course, this is what teachers and public service announcements have always told us: if we want our children to read, we must read. If we want them to read "substantive" material, we must do the same. In addition to modeling, the young reader has to find an individual or a community with which he or she can share the passion for reading.

But what about those passionate readers for whom reading was never modeled in the home? This second kind of reader Heath characterizes as:

> the social isolate—the child who from an early age felt very different from everyone around him. This is very, very difficult to uncover in an interview. People don't like to admit that they were social isolates as children. What happens is you take that sense of being different into an imaginary world. But that world, then, is a world you can't share with the people around you—because it's imaginary. And so the important dialogue in your life is with the *authors* of the books you read. Though they aren't present, they become your community. (77)

In other words, some readers, because of their felt sense of being unlike family and friends around them, turn to books for their sense of belonging and identity. Throughout their lives, these readers tend to turn to literature to make sense of their lives and to make sense of their difference and their perceptions of the world:

> With near-unanimity, Heath's respondents described substantive works of fiction as, she said, "the only places where there was some civic, public hope of coming to grips with the ethical, philosophical and sociopolitical dimensions of life that were elsewhere treated so simplistically. From Agamemnon forward, for example, we've been having to deal with the conflict between loyalty to one's family and loyalty to the state. And strong works of fiction are what refuse to give easy answers to the conflict, to paint things as black and white, good guys versus bad guys. They're everything pop psychology is not." (*Franzen* 82)

Heath's research reveals something of what so many readers go to literature to find and reveals something of how literature can become "addictive," providing a kind of "relationship" that many of us can find nowhere else in our lives. Franzen takes some comfort from Heath's research, yet at the same time that he is discomfited by the contemporary view of success as producing a "blockbuster" novel and by "book clubs for treating literature like a cruciferous vegetable that could be choked down only with a spoonful of socializing" (88), he also acknowledges, "Readers and writers are united in their need for solitude, in their pursuit of substance in a time of ever-increasing evanescence: in their reach inward, via print, for a way out of loneliness" (88).

What is ironic in Franzen's account of his struggle with despair and his growing understanding of what draws people to the kind of literature he works to produce is his much-publicized resistance to a cultural figure that is currently having more impact than anyone or any institution on the reading of serious fiction in this country: Oprah Winfrey. Although Heath describes two avenues individuals take to becoming lifelong, passionate readers, Winfrey offers a kind of third way to "serious" fiction that combines both avenues, a way that both models reading and offers a sense of community. Winfrey started her book club in 1996 as part of her popular talk show, and the response was phenomenal. The first book she selected, Jacqueline Pritchard's *Deep End of the Ocean*, almost immediately became a bestseller. In fact, throughout the life of the first manifestation of her Book Club from 1996 to 2002 and now in the second manifestation as she selects "classic" novels such as Steinbeck's *East of Eden* and Tolstoy's *Anna Karenina*, the books on her list sell extraordinarily well. Standard operating procedure for each book begins with Oprah's dramatic revelation on her show of the next selection. She divides the book into several "assignments" to give her audience goals to work for. She also tantalizes her Book Club members with brief "teasers" immediately before commercials during her show to keep them reading, such as one for *East of Eden* in which Winfrey asks, "Have you gotten to the big scene yet?" Winfrey now also offers a sophisticated Web site that provides a variety of pedagogical support, including biographical information and reading questions written by academics from such institutions as Williams College. When the club is reading more challenging books such as Gabriel Garcia Marquez's *One Hundred Years of Solitude* or Toni Morrison's *Beloved*, Winfrey encourages and cajoles her audience to keep plugging away and to complete each "assignment" because the end will be worth the effort. And, of course, the Book Club member wants to finish the book to feel a part of the reading "community" that comes together in the show that discusses the current selection, shows in which "real" people and celebrities (for example, Kelsey Grammer was on her show to discuss *East of Eden*) share their responses. In addition, Book Club members can purchase tee shirts, hats, and other paraphernalia advertising one's membership and Winfrey donates proceeds to various community literacy programs. Winfrey herself makes no money from the sale of Book Club merchandise or from the sale of the Book Club selections.

Whereas Winfrey has received widespread media attention for her successful promotion of literacy, she is not unique in her attempts to guide others' literacy practices. For example, Mortimer Adler's *How to Read a Book* has never been out of print since its first publication in 1940. Adler, along with Robert Hutchins, one of the founders of the Great Books Program, carries on in the Arnoldian tradition, which believes reading the right sorts of literature in the right sorts of ways is necessary to the health of both the individual and the culture. *How to Read a Book* includes chapters on how to read different types of books, how to approach an author, and how to criticize; it also includes a list of books worth reading, from Homer's *Iliad* and *Odyssey* to Aleksandr Solzhenitsyn's *Cancer Ward*, as well as tests (with answers) to judge the "success" of one's own reading. He offers the list because, he argues, "we can learn only from our 'betters.' We must know who they are and how to learn from them. The person who has this sort of knowledge possesses the art of reading in the sense with which we are especially concerned in this book" (10). Reading, in other words, is not to provide us with a sense of belonging or common ground but with a humble awareness of our lesser status. We go with hat in hand to learn from our "betters."

At the end of the 1972 edition, Adler writes, "Reading well, which means reading actively, is thus not only a good in itself, nor it is merely a means to advancement in our work or career. It also serves to keep our minds alive and growing" (346). I have to admit that I find Adler's instruction dry going. One reads through 346 pages of advice before getting to the list that leads one to begin to practice what Adler has preached. The pleasure to be derived from reading seems to be based on a desire for personal fulfillment and betterment. Yet following Adler's many instructions is daunting at best. The discussion of how to read analytically describes three distinct stages with each stage containing numerous rules. Adler will most likely not persuade anyone not already sold on the value of "keep[ing] our minds alive and growing." Yet, as I mentioned, his book has never been out of print since its initial publication. What is more alluring in Adler's project is the notion that he has indeed provided a list of books that mark one as well read. For those of us from working-class backgrounds or backgrounds that did not model a valuing of the humanities, we may find real comfort in possessing such a list that seems to promise the key to enter an elite world of ideas of which we desire to be a part. A desire to read *How to Read a Book* probably has more to do with the desire to be part of an intellectual community than to feel "our minds alive and growing."

A follower in Adler's footsteps is Clifton Fadiman, a scion of the Book of the Month Club whose *Lifetime Reading Plan* is dedicated to Adler. Like Adler, Fadiman holds an Arnoldian belief in reading as essential to a life well lived and makes a significant part of his career working to make literacy accessible and attractive to others. Also like Adler, Fadiman tries to lead others to literature, literature that is significant to Western culture. Reading, of course, is not a matter of passive reception for Fadiman any more than it is for Adler. Fadiman compares the reading of significant works of literature to marriage and family; in his "Preliminary Talk with the Reader," he writes that the benefit of reading the books listed in his plan "is rather like what is offered by loving and marrying, having and rearing children, carving out a career, creating a home. They can be a major experience, a source of continuous internal growth" (2). Yet his notion of family offers little by way of warmth as he goes on to describe his aim in providing this plan and what the plan makes available to those who undertake it:

> The Plan is designed to help us avoid mental bankruptcy. It is designed to fill our minds, slowly, gradually, under no compulsion, with what the greatest writers of our Western tradition have thought, felt, and imagined. Even after we have shared these thoughts, feelings, and images, we will still have much to learn: all men die uneducated. But at least we will not feel quite so lost, so bewildered. We will have disenthralled ourselves from the merely contemporary. We will understand something, not much but something, of our position in space and time. (2)

Imagining how the novice reader eager to undertake a "lifetime reading plan" might respond to "all men die uneducated" is difficult for me. Why is letting his readers know that, at the end of their lifetime of reading, they will "understand something, not much but something, of our position in space and history" so important for Fadiman? Why is humbling them as they begin important? And why continue when the rewards are represented in such a chilly fashion?

Equally cryptic is Fadiman's odd critique of the age in which he lives. He writes:

> living in an age which to its cost has abandoned the concept of the Hero, we
> will have acquired models of high thought and feeling. We will feel buoyed up
> by the noble stream of Western civilization of which we are a part. This book,
> then, is a small act of faith, faith in the notion that a great many Americans,
> despite all the pressures inducing them to do so, have no desire to remain
> All-American Boys and Girls. (2–3)

I admit that I have difficulty figuring out what he is referring to here. The book was first copyright in 1960 and again in 1976. If he were referring to the 1960s as a period of protest and rebellion, he would have no reason to refer to the "pressures" to "remain All-American Boys and Girls." I am also unaware of any distinct overt pressures for such ethnocentrism even in 1976, America's Bicentennial year. The only interpretation I can come up with is a response to cold war politics that questioned a wide-ranging intellect as potentially un-American. Yet still the tone seems oddly defensive.

Perhaps we can tell more specifically what he means by asking for whom he has created his plan. But his definition of audience is wide-ranging: "In general the Plan is meant for the American, from eighteen to eighty, who is curious to see what his mind can master in the course of his remaining lifetime, and who has not met more than ten percent, let us say, of the writers listed" (3), and he goes on to include everyone who, for whatever reasons, finds something missing from his or her life, an emptiness that great literature can begin to fill. Yet the Plan is not for the lazy. Fadiman states, "Reading is not a passive experience, except when you're reading trash or the news. It should be, and is, one of the most vigorous modes of living. A good book, like healthy exercise, can give you that pleasant sense of fatigue that comes of having stretched your mental muscles" (9–10). So, ultimately, the main reason to read serious literature is that it is good for you and that, like exercise, it will benefit you in the long run. And, again, as with Adler, Fadiman fails to perceive that his readers may desire a sense of being part of an intellectual community, and it is that sense of community that is a real source of pleasure and motivation, for example, I want to be someone who reads Hobbes' *Leviathan*, not knowing that I will die "uneducated" but that I am part of a community who knows who Hobbes is as opposed to a community who does not. There is an important distinction here.

Still another well-known literacy "guru" is Harold Bloom. He received considerable attention a decade ago with the publication of *The Western Canon*, his attempt to revitalize interest in "substantive" literature and reading. Bloom's

How to Read and Why is another effort to lead his audience to reading by guiding them through important examples from four literary genres—poetry, drama, novels, and short stories. An unabashed humanist who is utterly contemptuous of much contemporary critical practice, Bloom argues that reading connects us more firmly than any other activity to "life": "We read Shakespeare, Dante, Chaucer, Cervantes, Dickens, Proust, and all their peers because they more than enlarge life. Pragmatically, they have become the Blessing, in its true Yahwistic sense of 'more life into a time without boundaries'" (28). Indeed, Bloom's discussion of the pleasure to be found in reading reaches a kind of mystical plane where the reader "transcends" the quotidian. He describes the reading of "the now much-abused traditional canon" as the source of a "difficult pleasure," and he argues that " . . . a pleasurable difficulty seems to me a plausible definition of the Sublime" (29). This strikes me, despite my taking issue with his critical position, as a particularly powerful way to describe the way readers describe their experiences of feeling more in the world of the book than in the world around them and of our utter conviction that reading makes our lives "better" in ways that are both real and ineffable. Bloom goes on to describe the "reader's Sublime" as "the only secular transcendence we can ever attain, except for the even more precarious transcendence we call 'falling in love'" (29).

More than Adler or Fadiman, Bloom seems to capture something of the palpable pleasure a reader finds in a book that both challenges and satisfies. But, to be fair, all three (and these are only three of the many enthusiasts who have written books seeking to introduce the joys of literacy to others) sincerely wish to bring a wide audience to greater literacy, that is to a particular kind of literacy that challenges readers to engage actively with the meaning-making of reading rather than just turning the pages of a "page turner." Certainly, too, Bloom in particular has been met with resistance as he has made it something of his life's work to revalorize the Western Canon. Yet his work has received grudging respect from his opponents. Considering why Winfrey's efforts have been met with such a surprising degree of animosity as she attempts to participate in the same tradition as Adler, Fadiman, Bloom, and others is interesting. Jonathan Franzen's experience with Oprah's Book Club offers a way to begin that consideration.

In his essay "Why Bother?" Franzen writes of his growing awareness that "serious" novels no longer matter in the way that, say, *Catch-22* mattered and of his growing depression. He writes:

> You ask yourself, why am I bothering to write these books? I can't pretend the mainstream will listen to the news I have to bring. I can't pretend I'm subverting anything because any reader capable of decoding my subversive messages does not need to hear them (and the contemporary art scene is a constant reminder of how silly things get when artists start preaching to the choir). (73)

Franzen's concern is that he cannot affect society with his socially conscious and socially critical novels because his audience already knows whatever he has to say and the "mainstream" will not listen to his message. But, of course, Winfrey offered him exactly what he seems to be asking for here—a way to make the "mainstream" listen to his message and learn to "decode" the subversion he hopes for—when she selected his novel *The Corrections* for her Book Club. But rather than treating his selection as the opportunity it would seem to be, he recoiled; in fact, his response to being selected as an "Oprah author" became so contentious that he is the only "Oprah author" to be uninvited from the Book Club.

The Corrections, a long and challenging novel, tells the story of a difficult family. It is not a sentimental story of a family's coming together at the death of the patriarch; instead, it is remarkable in a sense for its very banality—the characters are middle-class white adults struggling with their needs and neuroses. The protagonist, Chip Lambert, a prickly thirty-something in a career nosedive, clearly draws from Franzen's own life and family. And one of Winfrey's standard Book Club moves is to ask authors to help her audience make connections with them and offer insights into how they may have made use of their own autobiographies, particularly helpful when the novel is not easy to read and when none of the characters is particularly sympathetic. Much of the novel is set in St. Louis, the elder Lamberts live in St. Louis as did Franzen's parents, and Franzen grew up in St. Louis, yet when asked to make any of the connections between his life and his novel explicit, he resists.

In his essay "Meet Me in St. Louis," originally published in the *New Yorker*, Franzen mercilessly emphasizes the "staginess" of the footage for the talk show shot in his hometown, and his resistance to providing anything personal for Winfrey's audience manifests itself in hives that torment him in each "up close and personal moment." To provide background for Winfrey's interview with him, Franzen is filmed driving very slowly over the bridge into St. Louis, standing under the Arch, looking at the tree he and his family planted at his father's death, and walking down the street in front of his childhood home. Ultimately, he explodes, "This is so fundamentally bogus!" (270). He can only imagine what is being asked of him as "schmaltz" (269). When he writes, "one of my friends will report that Winfrey said the author had poured so much into the book that 'he must not have a thought left in his head'" (272), he cannot hear Winfrey the rhetorician connecting with her audience; he can only hear her speaking on a literal level. Whereas he attempts to describe his "sense of dividedness" over the worthiness of Winfrey's work versus the "schmaltziness" of it, he wants to be taken seriously as a serious writer and fears that Winfrey's Book Club logo on the cover of his book would diminish his reputation.

Franzen is not alone in his discomfort. Winfrey's project is dismissed or reviled by many who assume that she selects sentimental, "schmaltzy," middlebrow material for middlebrow (female) readers. But the assumptions about what Winfrey is doing in her Book Club in both manifestations are problematic. Certainly, some of the selections for the Book Club have been less challenging, more overtly sentimental stories with predictable plots, but Winfrey balances her selections so that "easy" books are most likely to be followed by books such *The Corrections* or *Beloved* or *The Reader*—and, at this writing, a trio of William Faulkner novels. Why do Winfrey's detractors rarely mention the latter and focus on the former? Ted Striphas, in "A Dialectic with the Everyday: Communication and Cultural Politics on Oprah Winfrey's Book Club," contends that sexism plays a role in such dismissal: "Reproachful responses to Oprah's Book Club, in other words, provide a kind of cover under which are smuggled demeaning attitudes towards women and the cultural forms they tend to engage" (297). True, Winfrey tends to select books written by and for women, but her audience is overwhelmingly female. Women readers tend to value stories that focus on the complexities of relationships, yet these stories are quickly categorized as "schmaltz." Striphas argues:

> Indeed, the vociferous public outcry generated by Oprah's Book Club was and remains symptomatic of the club's challenge to a regime of cultural value that has consistently excluded, or at the very least marginalized, hundreds of thousands and perhaps millions of women/readers. Future research would do well to assess the extent to which communication on Oprah's Book Club has helped to construct a broader, creative, and politically progressive set of codes, vocabularies, and practices for these and other women and, if so, to chart their circulation in and beyond the *Oprah Winfrey Show*. (311)

Certainly, the discussion during episodes devoted to each book selection does not resemble a graduate seminar, but is that the model we wish to replicate?

In fact, as Rona Kaufman points out, Winfrey almost never mentions school or literature classes as part of Book Club discussions: "Oprah's Book Club . . . made no reference to school, and because the purpose of the club was to reunite literature (or literary fiction and nonfiction) with those who can read it but have chosen not to, that lack of reference points to the failure of a kind of academic reading for these club members" (225). For Oprah and her readers, reading is "transformative" and "relevant" (224); it is, in other words, very unlike reading done in many literature classes. However, the academy has largely ignored Winfrey's efforts at literacy education. In "The 'Oprahfication' of Literacy: Reading 'Oprah's Book Club,'" R. Mark Hall points out that "[a]lthough the influence of 'Oprah's Book Club' has been well documented in the popular media, it has received little attention from the academic community" (647). Winfrey's approach makes academics nervous or dismissive or both for several reasons. For one thing, Winfrey establishes her ethos as a person—a woman—whose life was saved by reading. She perfectly fits Heath's description of a reader born of having been a "social isolate" as she frequently

refers to her lonely, unloved childhood. Winfrey turned to books for comfort and love as a child and adolescent and wants to offer her audience that
same sense of comfort and belonging. Her desire to lead others to the pleasure
and transformative potential of reading is palpable; reading was a means to
self-discovery, self-help, and self-healing for her, and she believes it can be for
others as well. In addition, she generates a sense of community for those participating in the club—even when "participation" only means reading the book
and watching the program. Kaufman argues:

> What's important to notice is that Oprah's Book Club reenergized literacy,
> providing a forum for reading that is encouraging and that relies on a spirit
> of trust. The book club worked from the beginning to construct a particular
> readership—to value and enact a particular way of reading. By highlighting
> certain reading testimonies, celebrating and literally applauding them, by
> using Oprah as the model of success and usefulness of this form of literacy,
> the book club created its own culture of reading. (228)

Of course, what the viewer sees on the television program or reads on the Web
site is carefully edited, but at no point do we see Oprah or a reader denigrating
another. Reader responses are only respected—even when readers confess they
did not care for or could not finish the selection. The "culture of reading" is
only positive, only accepting.
    This "culture of reading" is unlike that in most literature classes, and both
Hall and Kaufman remark that the discursive practices on the show and the
Web site work hard not to sound like school. Hall, for example, points out,
"Though she may serve yellowtail tuna crusted with pistachios, followed by
herb-roasted pork with pea risotto [at her dinner party for Toni Morrison],
Winfrey is careful, nonetheless, not to construct her book as too highbrow"
(653). In other words, Winfrey, aware of how fragile women's intellectual egos
can be, strives to make sure no one feels that the discussion is over her head or
exclusionary. Kaufman, too, sees Winfrey positioning the club carefully on the
reading club model rather than the school model:

> The club's placement outside the academy allowed for freedom and flexibil-
> ity of participation. Simply put, it wasn't school. Membership was optional.
> There was no penalty for dropping out. Members could decide not to read
> and not to watch the book-club episodes with no penalty—other than a
> sense of being left out of a growing cultural conversation. (233)

Kaufman goes on to argue, however, that, in the discussion of Morrison's *Paradise*, Winfrey "moved the readers into an academic realm—literally, since the
meeting took place at Princeton, and figuratively, since the discussion used the
language of school and emphasized the cognitive over the emotive" (245). The
discussion took place in a classroom with Morrison as professor and Winfrey as

Good point [handwritten marginal note]

bright teaching assistant. Kaufman sees this move as "Oprah invading the Ivy League, claiming it as a legitimate space for nonelite readers. Along those same lines, her insistence on using the language of school, oversimplified though it was, may be seen [as] a kind of reclaiming of a credible studentship for adults" (246). As part of this reclamation, Kaufman further argues that Winfrey's influence can be said to go beyond getting many people excited about reading as well as making some writers (or writer's estates) wealthy:

> If we think about the ways in which Oprah constructed the meetings, the ways in which she authorized particular readings and comments, including her own, we can see her as the author of a canon—for herself and the millions of viewers who follow her. Her canon reversed usual hierarchies: black women are at the top, white men are at the bottom. (248)

Winfrey's canon valorizes the personal; books are supposed to touch as well as educate the reader, and the best books are those that bring those qualities together most ably, which may be why Morrison's work is at the peak of the Winfrey canon. And Winfrey herself becomes the quintessential teacher, guiding her "students" to (at least the potential for) individual fulfillment.

Winfrey sponsors the members of her reading club in the truest sense. As Deborah Brandt defines them, *sponsors* "are any agents, local or distant, concrete or abstract, who enable, support, teach, model, as well as recruit, regulate, suppress, or withhold literacy—and gain advantage by it in some way" (166). Winfrey prepared the way by establishing her own credibility and gaining the trust of her viewers; she cheers readers along, helping them continue reading long and difficult works such as *Anna Karenina* and *100 Years of Solitude*; she employs an impressive staff to provide reading support on her Web site. Most importantly, she makes readers feel good about being a part of something larger than themselves, and they are confident that they will never be made to feel bad about misreadings or failures to finish their reading. She never gives any tests. Reader and viewer testimonials—as well as continuing book sales— seem to indicate that Book Club members benefit from their participation and feel a real connection to Winfrey herself. Winfrey, too, gains "advantage" in the continuing success of her afternoon talk show and her resulting, much publicized wealth.

I am not arguing that educators should adopt Oprah's model, copying her methods and focusing on making students feel the reading and writing they do for us can transform their lives, but surely we can still learn from such success. For example, Hall writes, "Rather than denigrate the most pervasive form of communication in our culture, we ought to examine the literate behaviors associated with 'Oprah's Book Club' more closely, seeking ways to join television and print literacies" (664). Perhaps, too, he suggests, we should "consider . . . the ways that the classroom study of literature sometimes dims the joy of reading" (665). Kaufman also concludes her essay observing that educators would gain "from recognizing Oprah's Book Club as a significant and complicated site of reading, one that could have helped to concretize the idea that we read differently in different locations and that those acts of reading allow us to locate ourselves in a social world" (249). Of course, Winfrey does not have to grade her Book Club members on the jobs they do, and she is free from the kinds of accountability educators find themselves increasingly asked to provide, especially at state-supported institutions of higher learning. And if people stop reading her Book Club selections, she can end her reading club at any time—as she did briefly a couple of years ago. But, as Brandt points out, "Neither rich nor powerful enough to sponsor literacy on our own terms, we [teachers] serve instead as conflicted brokers between literacy's buyers and sellers" (183). And many educators are beginning to question literacy and literature's role in the current humanities curriculum.

Recall David Bleich's observation in "What Literature Is 'Ours'?" that "literature does not matter because its substance is considered interchangeable with similar substances available from a variety of media" (289). He draws from students and their responses to readings in a course he designed (and from which the title of the essay comes), and what he observes does not please him:

> Yet see how even intelligent, highly motivated, good-natured students struggle, how distant they feel from the language of the American literature they read. See how rarely they identify a literary idea with what actually exists in society. And these are American students reading American writers, writing about issues that implicate all American people. There is no culture gap. There is, however, the presupposition that literature and language do not matter: there is only the most distant sense that overtaking the language of literature and making it our own changes how we are as social figures. (311)

Bleich's students feel little connection with the texts they read in his class, texts that include Toni Morrison's *Sula* and Jane Smiley's *A Thousand Acres*. Winfrey's audience connected, however, with *Sula* and found the book not only meaningful, but they also were able to make connections to their own lives and to the cultural circumstances that produced Sula. What kinds of connections was Bleich looking for that his students could not produce?

Kurt Spellmeyer, too, in his recent book *Arts of Living: Reinventing the Humanities for the Twenty-First Century*, sees a failure of the humanities—particularly English departments—to connect with students' lives and argues that this failure has ramifications that extend far beyond the classroom. Like Bleich, he maintains that what is taught in English classes is largely disconnected from culture itself and that not only do students not see the point of studying the humanities, neither do the faculty members teaching these courses.

Spellmeyer writes, "The humanities are in trouble because they have become increasingly isolated from the life of the larger society" (4).

Humanists such as Clifton Fadiman and Harold Bloom cite the influences of mass media and a corporate mindset that value profit over everything else as major sources in the decline of the humanities, but Spellmeyer argues that the humanities participated in their own decline in a process that has taken well over a century. In the nineteenth century, for example, literary societies were integral parts of middle-class social life, from debating societies in the colleges and universities to women's clubs that featured essays their members wrote and presented:

> The denigration of mass culture allowed scholars . . . to wrest literary art from the undergraduate reading societies, a fixture of academic life since Ralph Waldo Emerson's time, and from the even more successful women's clubs operating outside the university. But these founders were less successful in defining what it was about the literary work of art that required such careful handling. (77)

As education and career preparation became more and more professionalized, faculty in the humanities—particularly in literature—also had to specialize, "developing a 'scientific' form of historical scholarship modeled on German criticism and philology," giving "English and other humanities both a methodology and a quasi-scientific image" (77). Spellmeyer sees these nineteenth-century changes as part of a progression of knowledge specialization that has ultimately resulted in the isolation of the humanities from culture at large. In the contemporary academy, he sees the current manifestation of that specialization as being the "practice of critique," which he metaphorically describes as "illness" (145).

In a similar vein, Bill Readings points to the increasingly administrative function of teaching and argues that the university is a "ruined institution" (152). In *The University in Ruins*, he seeks:

> to perform a structural diagnosis of contemporary shifts in the University's function as an institution, in order to argue that the wider social role of the University as an institution is now up for grabs. It is no longer clear what the place of the university is within society nor what the exact nature of that society is, and the changing institutional form of the University is something that intellectuals cannot afford to ignore. (2)

Readings argues that the growing corporatization of the university can be seen as the creeping influence of concepts taken from corporate strategies—particularly the peculiar use the adherents of Total Quality Management make of the concept of *excellence*. Both argue that these movements serve to separate teacher from student, student from culture, and school from culture.

So Spellmeyer argues that we must "free" ourselves from critique, and Readings argues that we must resist pernicious influences of the corporate world. How are we to achieve these goals? Spellmeyer calls for a "pragmatics" of reading by which he means "ways of reading that restore a sense of connection to things, and with it, a greater confidence in our ability to act" (168). He writes, "The rarification of the arts—their sequestration from everyday life and their metamorphosis into objects of abstruse expert consumption—typifies the very essence of disenchanted society as Weber described it and this development corresponds quite closely to other forms of political and social disenfranchisement" (195). In other words, literature as the preserve of a specially-trained elite is emblematic of a generalized separation of "ordinary people" from sites and seats of power. Instead, for Spellmeyer, the university and, more specifically, the humanities have a responsibility to "offer people freedom, and beyond that, to express real solidarity with the inner life of ordinary citizens" (223).

Readings, on the other hand, argues that teachers must begin to perceive themselves and to speak of themselves in the terms of the rhetor as opposed to the magister, that is, as "a speaker who takes account of the audience" rather than a speaker who "is indifferent to the specificity of his or her addressees" (158), and he reminds us that the etymological root of *education* is the Latin *e ducere*, or to draw out. He maintains ultimately, "the University will have to become one place, among others, where the attempt is made to think the social bond without recourse to a unifying idea, whether of culture or of the state" (191). The disciplines obviously do not offer such a place because, for Readings, their attempts to structure knowledge have greatly contributed to the problems he sees in the contemporary university. Readings also makes clear that the end of such thinking cannot be determined. The direction of true dialogue, such as he calls for, cannot be controlled or predicted if it is to become a vital place within a culture.

Spellmeyer concludes that "[o]ur job is not to lead but to prepare and to support" (245), and I am struck that we have a model who works "to prepare and to support" as well as to "draw out"—Oprah Winfrey. Rona Kaufman, too, sees a "missed opportunity." She writes, "If Spellmeyer were to look beyond his framework—look outside the university now—he could see, in the abundance of reading publics, models of experiential reading already in existence. And he might find both comfort and instruction in seeing through that different lens" (223). I agree, but I want to make clear that I am not calling for a full-scale embracing of unfiltered expressivism (although I am also aware of how my argument can be read this way). For one thing, as Anne J. Herrington and Marcia Curtis make clear in *Persons in Process: Four Stories of Writing and Personal Development in College*, few students come to college to express themselves; they come to college to learn a repertoire of strategies for expressing themselves:

"Though they all [the four students in their study], in their own diverse ways, speak of the desire for 'self-expression,' they are not what we might call 'self-content'"(4). They continue, "All four students speak of the wish, the tendency, to write from personal experience toward something more public, toward essays addressed to an audience capable of understanding and for a kindred group capable of identifying with them" (5). Additionally, sometimes students have to be pushed to dig more deeply into complex ideas in their reading and writing, and that sort of work is not what we generally hear when we hear the phrase *self-expression*. But just as Winfrey can push and convince her audience that continuing to read Morrison's *Paradise* or *Song of Solomon* or Marquez's *100 Years of Solitude* is worth the effort, we can find ways to convince our students to engage meaningfully with the assignments we compose for them. And we can turn to Winfrey to assess her methods and consider which of them could transfer to the college classroom. What can we learn from Winfrey as she provides a safe place to talk about difficult issues such as race, class, gender identity, sexism, and religion? What can we learn from her carefully constructed Web site entries that accompany each book? What can we learn from her discursive style that strives to make readers feel comfortable? How might we learn from her pedagogical approaches to bring an element of pleasure back in the classroom? And how might we make use of stories to help our students learn and connect to the work they do in our classrooms?

We need to find ways in the classroom to capture and provide a sense of invitation and community. In a sense, we need to come up with a mission statement that acknowledges how we read and write for many complex reasons and considers how pleasure must play a role—not the only role, just a role—in our own learning as well as in our teaching. As I have argued earlier herein, we cannot assume that our students hold the same attitudes toward higher literacy as ours. They may not come from homes where literate practices were "heavily modeled," and, fortunately for them, most were not "social isolates" who turned to books for "salvation" or escape. But we cannot know what our students' attitudes are without dialogue—*real* dialogue. As Elizabeth Chiseri-Strater writes:

> Academic discourse communities cannot flourish without real dialogue, without engaged reading, without committed writing, without an extension of the private literacies that are an inherent part of many students who inhabit our classrooms. We must allow ourselves to integrate into our classrooms those literacy/learning practices that will enable students both to belong to and participate in many discourse communities during their university careers and finally in their lifetimes. (167)

Having studied the literate practices of two students in and out of the classroom, Chiseri-Strater helps us see how even well-meaning teachers can make assumptions that work against our students, expecting them to, in essence, read our minds. She, like Readings, calls for dialogue—"real dialogue." But that dialogue cannot "flourish" without back-and-forth, give-and-take, without consideration of where and how our students find pleasure in their reading and writing and pleasure in their abilities to connect the reading and writing they do to their lives.

Throughout this book, I have argued that reading and writing matter to us for complex and complicated reasons. Some of us are drawn to reading and writing even though sociological factors predict the opposite. Others of us assume that all have the same access to and assumptions about reading and writing that we did and do. My research here indicates that, in all likelihood, our students will not share our attitudes and assumptions, but as teachers our responsibility is to model reading and writing practices for our students, to learn something of their literacy backgrounds, and to consider how we may learn of avenues to explore from diverse sources, such as our own and others' literacy narratives or a charismatic figure such as Oprah Winfrey. The goal ultimately is to become more conscious of the jobs we do as literacy sponsors and to learn more about what our students desire from their moves to "higher literacy."

Works Cited

Abbott, H. Porter. *The Cambridge Introduction to Narrative*. Cambridge, Eng.: Cambridge UP, 2002.

Adler, Mortimer. *How to Read a Book*. 1940. New York: MJF Books, 1972.

Alger, Horatio. *Ragged Dick, and Mark, the Match Boy*. New York: Colliers, 1962.

Althusser, Louis. "Ideology and Ideological State Apparatuses (Notes towards an Investigation." *Lenin and Philosophy*. New York: Monthly Review, 1971.

Arnove, Robert F., and Harvey J. Graff. "National Literacy Campaigns." *Literacy: A Critical Sourcebook*. Ed. Ellen Cushman, Eugene R. Kintgen, Barry M. Kroll, and Mike Rose. Boston: Bedford/St. Martin's, 2001. 591–615.

Awkward, Michael. *Scenes of Instruction: A Memoir*. Durham, NC: Duke UP, 1999.

Banks, William P. "Written through the Body: Disruptions and 'Personal' Writing." *College English* 66 (2003): 21–40.

Bartholomae, David. "Inventing the University." *When a Writer Can't Write: Studies in Writer's Block and Other Composing-Process Problems*. Ed. Mike Rose. New York: Guilford, 1985. 134–65.

Bartholomae, David, and Anthony Petrosky. *Facts, Artifacts, and Counterfacts: Theory and Method for a Reading and Writing Course*. Portsmouth, NH: Heinemann, 1986.

———. *Ways of Reading*, 6th ed. Boston: Bedford/St. Martin's, 2002.

Berger, John. *Ways of Seeing*. New York: Penguin, 1995.

Bjorkland, Diane. *Interpreting the Self: Two Hundred Years of American Autobiography*. Chicago: U of Chicago P, 1998.

Bleich, David. "What Literature Is 'Ours'?" Schweickart and Flynn 286–313.

Bloom, Allan. *The Closing of the American Mind*. New York: Simon & Schuster, 1988.

Bloom, Harold. *How to Read and Why*. New York: Simon, 2000.

Bowles, Samuel, and Herbert Gintis. *Schooling in Capitalist America: Educational Reform and the Contradictions of Economic Life*. New York: Basic, 1976.

Boylan, Jennifer. *She's Not There: A Life in Two Genders*. New York: Broadway, 2003.

Bragg, Rick. *All Over But the Shoutin.'* New York: Pantheon, 1997.

Brandt, Deborah. *Literacy in American Lives.* Cambridge, Eng.: Cambridge UP, 2001.

———. "Protecting the Personal." *College English* 64 (2001): 42–44.

———. "Sponsors of Literacy." *College Composition and Communication* 49 (1998): 165–85.

Brandt, Deborah et al. "The Politics of the Personal: Storying Our Lives against the Grain." *College English* 64 (2001): 41–62.

Brodkey, Linda. "Writing on the Bias." *College English* 56 (1994): 527–47.

Bruner, Jerome. *The Culture of Education.* Cambridge, MA: Harvard UP, 1996.

———. "Life as Narrative." *Social Research* 71 (2004): 691–710.

Chiseri-Strater, Elizabeth. *Academic Literacies: The Public and Private Discourse of University Students.* Portsmouth, NH: Boynton/Cook, 1991.

Coles, Gerald. *Reading the Naked Truth: Literacy, Legislation, and Lies.* Portsmouth, NH: Heinemann, 2003.

Coles, Robert E. *The Call of Stories: Teaching and the Moral Imagination.* Boston: Houghton, 1989.

Collins, James, and Richard Blot. *Literacy and Literacies: Texts, Power, and Identity.* Cambridge, Eng.: Cambridge UP, 2003.

Conley, Dalton. *Pecking Order: Which Siblings Succeed and Why.* New York: Pantheon, 2004.

De Lauretis, Teresa. *Alice Doesn't: Feminism, Semiotics, Cinema.* Bloomington: Indiana UP, 1984.

Dickerson, Debra. *An American Story.* New York: Pantheon, 2000.

Dijkstra, Bram. *Evil Sisters: The Threat of Female Sexuality and the Cult of Manhood.* New York: Knopf, 1996.

Douglass, Frederick. *Frederick Douglass: The Narrative and Selected Writings.* 1845. Ed. Michael Meyer. New York: Modern Library, 1984.

———. *Life and Times of Frederick Douglass.* 1881. New York: Macmillan, 1962.

Dunbar-Ortiz, Roxanne. *Red Dirt: Growing Up Okie.* New York: Verso, 1998.

Elder, Dana C. "Opinion: Different Climbs." *College English* 56 (1994): 568–70.

Evans, Mary. *Missing Persons: The Impossibility of Auto/Biography.* London: Routledge, 1999.

Fadiman, Anne. *Ex Libris: Confessions of a Common Reader.* New York: Farrar, 1998.

Fadiman, Clifton. *The Lifetime Reading Plan.* Cleveland, OH: World, 1976.

Faigley, Lester. *Fragments of Rationality: Postmodernity and the Subject of Composition.* Pittsburgh, PA: U of Pittsburgh P, 1993.

Finn, Patrick J. *Literacy with an Attitude: Educating Working-Class Children in Their Own Self-Interest.* Albany: State University of New York P, 1999.

Foucault, Michel. "Power and Strategies." *Power/Knowledge.* New York: Pantheon, 1980. 134–45.

———. "Truth and Power." *Power/Knowledge*. 109–33.

Franzen, Jonathan. *The Corrections*. New York: Farrar, 2001.

———. "Meet Me in St. Louis." *How to Be Alone: Essays*. New York: Farrar, 2002. 258–74.

———. "Why Bother?" *How to Be Alone: Essays*. 55–97.

Freire, Paulo. *Pedagogy of the Oppressed*. New York: Continuum International Publishing Group, 2000.

Gee, James Paul. *Social Linguistics and Literacies: Ideology in Discourses*. London: Falmer, 1990.

Geertz, Clifford. "Deep Play: Notes on the Balinese Cockfight." *The Interpretation of Cultures: Selected Essays*. New York: Basic, 1973.

Gere, Anne Ruggles. "Articles of Faith." *College English* 64 (2001): 46–47.

Glaspell, Susan. *A Jury of Her Peers. Plays*. Cambridge, New York: Cambridge UP, 1987.

Gramsci, Antonio. *Selections from the Prison Notebooks*. Trans. and ed. Quintin Hoare and Geoffrey Nowell Smith. New York: International, 1971.

Grimm, Nancy Maloney. *Good Intentions: Writing Center Work for Postmodern Times*. Portsmouth, NH: Boynton/Cook, 1999.

Hall, R. Mark. "The 'Oprahfication' of Literacy: Reading "Oprah's Book Club."" *College English* 65 (2003): 646–67.

Hamilton, Sharon Jean. *My Name's Not Susie: A Life Transformed by Literacy*. Portsmouth, NH: Boynton/Cook, 1995.

Harris, Joseph. "The Idea of Community in the Study of Writing." *College Composition and Communication* 40 (1989): 11–22.

Heath, Shirley Brice. *Ways with Words: Language, Life, and Work in Communities and Classrooms*. Cambridge, Eng.: Cambridge UP: 1983.

Herrington, Anne. "When Is My Business Your Business?" *College English* 64 (2001): 47–49.

Herrington, Anne J., and Marcia Curtis. *Persons in Process: Four Stories of Writing and Personal Development in College*. Urbana, IL: NCTE, 2000.

Hesford, Wendy. *Framing Identities: Autobiography and the Politics of Pedagogy*. Minneapolis: U of Minnesota P, 1999.

Hillocks, George. *The Testing Trap: How State Writing Assessments Control Learning*. New York: Teachers College P, 2002.

Hirsch, E. D. *Cultural Literacy: What Every American Needs to Know*. New York: Vintage, 1988.

hooks, bell. *Talking Back: Thinking Feminist, Thinking Black*. Boston: South End P, 1989.

———. *Teaching to Transgress: Education as the Practice of Freedom*. New York: Routledge, 1994.

Horner, Bruce, and Min-Zhan Lu. *Representing the "Other": Basic Writers and the Teaching of Basic Writing*. Urbana, IL: NCTE, 1999.

Hourigan, Maureen. *Literacy as Social Exchange: Intersections of Class, Gender, and Culture*. Albany: State University of New York P, 1994.

Hull, Glynda, and Mike Rose. "'This Wooden Shack Place': The Logic of an Unconventional Reading." *College Composition and Communication* 41 (1990): 287–98.

Il Postino. Dir. Michael Radford. Miramax, 1995.

Johnson, T. R. "School Sucks." *College Composition and Communication* 52 (2001): 620–50.

Kaufman, Rona. "'That, My Dear, Is Called Reading': Oprah's Book Club and the Construction of a Readership." Schweickart and Flynn 221–54.

Kirsch, Gesa. "Negotiating the Personal, the Private, and the Professional." *College English* 64 (2001): 55–57.

Lakoff, George, and Mark Johnson. *Metaphors We Live By*. Chicago: U of Chicago P, 1980.

Lareau, Annette. *Unequal Childhoods: Class, Race, and Family Life*. Berkeley: U of California P, 2003.

Lu, Min-Zhan. "Redefining the Legacy of Mina Shaughnessy." Horner and Lu 105–16.

Lubrano, Alfred. *Limbo: Blue-Collar Roots, White-Collar Dreams*. Hoboken, NJ: Wiley, 2004.

Mamet, David. *Oleanna*. New York: Vintage, 1992.

Marcus, Laura. *Auto/biographical Discourses: Theory, Criticism, Practice*. Manchester, Eng.: Manchester UP, 1994.

Miller, Richard E. "Fault Lines in the Contact Zone." *College English* 56 (1994): 389–419.

———. "Why Bother with Writing?" *College English* 64 (2001): 49–50.

Milner, Andrew. *Class*. London: Sage, 1999.

Office Space. Dir. Mike Judge. 20th Century Fox, 1999.

Oleanna. Dir. David Mamet. Perf. William H. Macy and Debra Eisenstadt. MGM/UA Video, 1994.

Pekar, Harvey. *American Splendor: The Life and Times of Harvey Pekar*. New York: Ballentine, 2003.

Pratt, Mary Louise. "Arts of the Contact Zone." *Ways of Reading*. Ed. Anthony Petrosky and David Bartholomae. 4th ed. Boston: Bedford/St. Martin's, 1996. 528–48.

Quindlen, Anna. *How Reading Changed My Life*. New York: Ballantine, 1998.

Readings, Bill. *The University in Ruins*. Cambridge, MA: Harvard UP, 1996.

Rodriguez, Richard. *Hunger of Memory: An Autobiography*. New York: Bantam, 1982.

Rose, Mike. *Lives on the Boundary*. New York: Penguin, 1989.

———. *The Mind at Work: Valuing the Intelligence of the American Worker.* New York: Viking, 2004.

———. *Possible Lives.* New York: Penguin, 1999.

Rowe, Paul L. *Reading Richard Rodriguez's* Hunger of Memory: *A Dialogic Review of the Criticism from the Perspective of a Working-Class Academic.* Diss. U of Houston, 1997.

Schroeder, Christopher. *ReInventing the University: Literacies and Legitimacy in the Postmodern Academy.* Logan, UT: Utah State UP, 2001.

Schwartz, Lynne Sharon. *Ruined by Reading: A Life in Books.* Boston: Beacon, 1996.

Schweickart, Patrocinio P., and Elizabeth A. Flynn, eds. *Reading Sites: Social Difference and Reader Response.* New York: MLA, 2004.

Scott, Joan W. "Experience." *Feminists Theorize the Political.* Ed. Judith Butler and Joan W. Scott. New York: Routledge, 1992. 23–38.

Scribner, Sylvia. "Literacy in Three Metaphors." *Perspectives on Literacy.* Ed. Eugene R. Kintgen, Barry M. Kroll, and Mike Rose. Carbondale: Southern Illinois UP, 1988. 71–81.

Shannon, Patrick. *Text, Lies, and Videotape: Stories about Life, Literacy, and Learning.* Portsmouth, NH: Heinemann, 1995.

Smith, Sidonie, and Julia Watson. *Reading Autobiography: A Guide for Interpreting Life Narratives.* Minneapolis: U of Minnesota P, 2002.

Smith, Valerie. *Self-Discovery and Authority in Afro-American Narrative.* Cambridge, MA: Harvard UP, 1987.

Smitherman, Geneva. *Talkin' and Testifyin': The Language of Black America.* Detroit: Wayne State UP, 1986.

Soliday, Mary. "Translating Self and Difference through Literacy Narratives." *College English* 56 (1994): 511–26.

Solomon, Andrew. "The Closing of the American Book." http://www.nytimes.com/2004/07/10/opinion/10SOLO.html?ex=1090475265&ei=1&en=7ae5489ad2571c8c. A17, col. 1.

Spellmeyer, Kurt. *Arts of Living: Reinventing the Humanities for the Twenty-First Century.* Albany: State University of New York P, 2003.

Spigelman, Candace. "Argument and Evidence in the Case of the Personal." *College English* 64 (2001): 63–87.

Steedman, Caroline. *Landscape for a Good Woman.* New Brunswick, NJ: Rutgers UP: 1986.

Street, Brian V. *Literacy in Theory and Practice.* Cambridge, Eng.: Cambridge UP, 1984.

Striphas, Ted. "A Dialectic with the Everyday: Communication and Cultural Politics on Oprah Winfrey's Book Club." *Cultural Studies in Media Communication* 20 (2003): 295–316.

Tompkins, Jane. *A Life in School: What the Teacher Learned*. Reading, PA: Addison Wesley, 1996.

Trimmer, Joseph. *Narration as Knowledge: Tales of the Teaching Life*. Portsmouth, NH: Boynton/Cook, 1997.

Villanueva, Victor. *Bootstraps: From an American Academic of Color*. Urbana, IL: NCTE, 1993.

Wray, Matt, and Annalee Newitz. *White Trash: Race and Class in America*. New York: Routledge, 1997.

Index

10945523R0

Made in the USA
Lexington, KY
03 September 2011